Giuseppe Scuto

Time for Action

*Securing Our Common Wealth
and Future*

Contents

Strange Fruit

History is the chronicle of the accumulation process.

1. Traditionally, history begins with the appearance of writing and this is a fact that, whether justifiable or conventional, is unintentionally also extremely symbolic. Contrary to what one might expect, the first written records in fact have nothing to do with myth, magic, religion or art – far from it. It's plain bookkeeping.

In fact, writing, and with it history, was born in the earliest cities and small kingdoms of mankind and arose from the need to record and keep an eye on how many animals are owned, on how many seeds, fruits, artifacts accumulate in the warehouses, on what enters them and what leaves them. Writing arises from the need to manage and control exchanges that go beyond the daily needs and quantities so large as to escape the human mind.

The natural need to safeguard one's family from the uncertainties of the future by stocking up on what can be put aside has transformed over time into a phenomenon with new and hitherto unmatched dimensions: accumulation as an end in itself, no longer limited by the survival needs in the short or medium term. And where the accumulation of goods transcends the sphere of everyday life and of the family, the need arises for a new technology capable of dealing with quantities and tasks never faced before. Writing is the answer to this need, a technology based on the use of conventional signs and entrusted to the first bureaucratic structure in history, the elite of scribes, with the task of controlling and administering the assets of the temple, of the landed aristocracy, of kings or pharaohs.

The beginning of history thus coincides with the moment in which accumulation transcends the familiar and everyday environment to become an urban and proto-state phenomenon. And, since the beginning, the accumulating machine already has in itself everything it needs to grow from century to century, everything that will characterize it to this day: an ideological system and the power to justify and defend itself, a technology that allows it and an apparatus of diligent technocrats who place themselves at its service. Today's world is nothing but the result and continuation of a process that began over 5,000 years ago with a few ingenious scratches in the soft clay.

> And there was evening and there was morning.
> (Genesis)

2. Differences in family and social roles have probably existed since the dawn of time. But, as long as large families of human beings lived in informal and mostly nomadic groups, their structures were still mobile and the differences within them were still attributable to the skills, ability, physical strength and courage of the various individuals.

With the consolidation of nomadic and semi-nomadic structures and communities into increasingly better defined and delimited tribes and peoples, the differences have gradually become institutionalized, acquiring such stability as to become rigid, if not even hereditary, and to create classes and castes within proto-state structures. With the development of agriculture, when the first permanent settlements saw the light, this social revolution had already taken place: the tasks of providing for the various needs of the first urban agglomerations – supply, production, government, defense – had already been distributed among the different community members, and social needs had already become predominant over the autonomy of individual family groups. This diversification of occupations, tasks and wages was at the origin of a substantial social differentiation and a consequent unequal division of resources and powers. But, unlike the long preceding millennia, social differentiation was this time, and for the first time in history, an institutionalized differentiation. Such an organizational leap was, for the community as a whole, progress. It allowed it to better protect itself, to have and achieve more. But not every single individual benefited equally. Depending on sex and class, what some gained in this revolution was in fact paid for dearly by others.

Having left the family environment and having become a communal, and therefore also political, phenomena, the accumulation of resources and differentiation of roles started to be the engine of the history of humanity which, in turn, was (and remains) substantially a chronicle of the process of accumulation and of the fight for it. The search for ever new opportunities for growth and accumulation has to this day been the dominant motive of every collective, political human event. It has always been a search and a tendency pursued by means of marriages and divorces, of alliances and betrayals, of aggressions and migrations in which the fortune or misfortune of kings and churches, masters, lords, slaves and poor people, as well as of every single individual on earth, has been dictated by the ability to accumulate resources, to know how to defend them, or by their ruinous loss. It is certainly no coincidence that the early civilizations in history, in Mesopotamia and Egypt, were characterized not only by a high organizational and technological level, but also by superior military technology, by the ability to start and win wars and by an inexhaustible push to conquer and expand to the detriment of neighboring peoples.

In all this, since the dawn of history, the accumulation mechanisms have never changed; only the historical circumstances in which they took place and the names that they have assumed in the different historical phases have. In a general sense, however, all these mechanisms can be reduced to only two categories: the subjugation of men and the appropriation of resources.

The natural price of labour is that price which is necessary to enable the labourers, one with another, to subsist and to perpetuate their race, without either increase or diminution.
(David Ricardo, *On the Principles of Political Economy and Taxation*)

3. Enslavement, the subjection of the other to one's will and to one's ends, is essential to the accumulation process. Indeed, it alone allows that multiplication of results which leads to an accumulation that goes beyond what is possible for a single individual, or a single family unit, in the course of an entire life.

The economies of classical Greece and Rome were entirely based on the use of slaves as a labor force. Before and after those civilizations, subjugation was based on the capture of enemy populations or the enslavement of human beings deemed inferior. It took the form of medieval serfdom, of the slavery in the American plantations, of the proletarian masses in the factories of the nineteenth and twentieth centuries. But whatever historical form it has taken, its logic has always remained the same and is the basis of the dynamic between slave and master, between servant and lord, between worker and employer. Moreover, far from being only a hierarchical relationship of an economic nature between social groups, subjection has always had an intra-family form, especially where patriarchal social models have always entailed a disparity between genders, ages and opportunities within each single family.

Given the antiquity of such a mechanism, it is not surprising that its modalities have always remained the same: physical coercion, subjection resulting from violence and unequal power relations, ideological entrapment, wherever individuals consider their enslavement a just and inherent fact in human nature or divine laws, blackmail and corruption, where individuals or entire social groups place themselves at the service of another by submitting to his wishes. Common to all these methods is alienation, i.e. the forced (dictated by the needs of mere subsistence) or voluntary (in exchange for privileges and advantages) transfer to the owner, lord or employer of a part of the value created with one's own work.

Evident throughout the evolution of history, these accumulation mechanisms have taken on a very particular, exemplary significance at certain historical moments. This is the case of the triangular trade, in which men and women captured in Africa were first reduced to merchandise, sold and bought, and then employed as working animals in America. Their masters could thus export their raw products to Europe where, starting with the materials arrived from the colonies, quality goods were produced that were sold around the world and which served, among other things, to finance the capture and purchase of more slaves. As sad and infamous as it is, such a trade is but one historical example among many. Thus also the pyramids of Egypt, in addition to being one of the seven wonders of the world, are above all the eternal monument to the exploitation and enslavement of thousands of human beings who, forced to build them, had to sacrifice freedom, dignity and life, reduced to an intermediate step between animal and man. Each block that composes them is the millennial testimony of the hundreds of existences that were consumed in oppression to place them where we admire them today.

Slavery is perhaps the most hateful historical institution through which masses of human beings have been deprived of their freedom, and often also of their lives, for the well-being and interest of their masters, so that they could accumulate riches upon riches and live a comfortable life far above the living conditions of their contemporaries.

And if this was the rationale for slavery among the Egyptians, Greeks and Romans, where it was a pillar of the economic system (i.e. of the accumulative processes) and was considered as natural as it was obvious and necessary, this was also the root cause of slavery in the Islamic kingdoms of the Middle Ages, the motive behind medieval serfdom and even the logic of a large part of today's labor market, formal or informal as it may be. Slavery, formally abolished almost everywhere as the forthright possession of living bodies, has never ceased to exist in the sense of coercion (physical or economic) and exploitation of the work of other human beings. So even today the world is full of men forced, in order to survive, to accept a job that consumes them and uses them until they are too old to still be useful. The number of those who, with their daily work, contribute to the accumulation of wealth of others is today greater than ever. The only difference is that today the boss has made himself less visible and that he only indirectly, that is, as an anonymous capitalist collectivity, has the power of life or death.

Excluding those societies still based on feudal and patronal economic models – not an insignificant number if one looks beyond the borders of industrialized nations – where he still has a face and a name known to all, the owner for whom one must work today, for whom one is often consumed to the point of exhaustion and for whom one even today at times dies, is a joint stock company, a distant, almost immaterial corporation difficult to hold to its responsibilities for what happens in the real life of the fields, of the factories and the offices.

The pyramids to which billions of today's workers laboriously carry their stones every day are no longer visible from afar, magnificent forms emerging on the horizon in the glory of the pharaoh. They are rather financial empires concealed behind complex legal constructs whose bank accounts, the very material of which today's pyramids are built, are jealously hidden from the view of most, fortunes guarded by law firms as well paid as they are unscrupulous, treasures buried in tax havens with exotic names or in virtual coffers in the heart of Europe.

> It is obvious that some are free men by nature, while other are slaves. And it is obvious that the latter are slaves for a just reason.
> (Aristotle, *Politics*)

4. Together with the enslavement of other human beings, the second mechanism of the historical process of accumulation relies on the appropriation of resources, i.e. on the conquest and hoarding of material resources available either because they can be subtracted from their owners or because they are not yet owned by someone. Along this line, man has since prehistoric times plundered his fellow men and even more so nature, understood as a complex of living and non-living beings, of everything that could be converted into value. Wealth and earning opportunities have been taken from enemy peoples or classes, fertile land has been taken from the forests, animals have been hunted, fished, bred or domesticated to feed and serve man in his work, or simply eliminated if an obstacle, an impediment to its free development. Minerals have been extracted from the bowels of the earth, wood and stone have served as building materials for boats, houses, roads, bridges and fortifications. This continuous hoarding of natural resources, however, has not only taken place at the expense of the forms of life that share the earth with us, but it has also been a plundering of man by man. Even where human voracity has not directly hurled itself towards the property of others, those who plundered nature in fact took possession of resources

potentially available to the entire community of men, subtracting them from it to make themselves their only master.

Such a scramble for resources, which began thousands of years ago, perhaps found its most emblematic historical expression in nineteenth- and twentieth-century colonialism and imperialism. In these historical phases, the competition between economic groups and the lack of scruples about the imposition of their own interests on those of others have shown their hardest face. Wars, conquests, subjugation and destruction of peoples and cultures, plundering of resources and goods, occupations of lands, impositions of corvée and tributes, deprivation of freedom for entire populations, forced labor ... everything happened in plain sight, with an arrogance, an indecency and a violence still astonishing to us today.

But, as in the case of the slave trade, the historical period of colonialism and imperialism is only a particular moment in a process that has always been going on. Since the beginning of history the first kingdoms and the first advanced civilizations have been able to develop only thanks to their own power to expand at the cost of others, often thanks to superior military technology (better metals for weapons, cavalry, war chariots), to superior organi-

16

zation or to the simple availability of larger armies. And, even later, the ferocious medieval wars in Europe, the arrival of peoples from Asia, the thrust of the conquistadors in Latin America or of the American pioneers towards the West were phenomena always attributable to the same, single need: to expand, acquire, conquer, obtain. To get more.

The contemporary versions of such a tendency are represented by today's neo- and postcolonialism, neo-imperialism and the subjugation by political or financial means in terms of alliances and agreements between unequal parties. Apparently free means of cooperation between sovereign countries, such agreements are far too often based on economic disparity and ultimately rest on a military power which is the last barely concealed foundation of all expansion and appropriation. Over a hundred years of history, the empires and their colonies have been replaced by commercial treaties and political-military alliances which, very often, go only to the advantage of the most powerful partner and the corrupt local elites, with the result of a net transfer of resources, and therefore value, from poorer to richer countries. Truly nothing new under the sun.

Let a prince conquer and hold the state, the means
will always be considered honest and be praised.
(Niccolò Machiavelli, *The Prince*)

5. The enslavement of the other and the
appropriation of resources on a large scale would
be impossible in a society of equals. What makes
accumulation possible is the difference in power
between men, families, social groups and nations.
History, as a chronicle of the accumulation process,
is therefore also and always the history of the struggle for power, that is, for dominance over others.

The physical and technological superiority and
the aggressiveness of an individual, a group or a
civilization were at the same time the beginning
and the foundation of a differentiation which, starting in prehistory, continued in historical times with
the military ideological and institutional subjugation of others. Religions and ideologies have always
been created and used by the historical structures
of power (aristocracies, priestly classes, ethnic
groups, social classes or patriarchal structures) and
their only purpose has always been to shape the entire social body at will, to convince it that a certain
inequality, indeed that very inequality that allow
those who hold the power to maintain it, is natural,

necessary or convenient, if not even an expression of the divine will.

What consolidates such a step is therefore institutional subjugation, aimed at fixing the power relations between individuals and social groups in a system that is rigid enough to guarantee that the desired form of social inequality is perpetuated over time and that the imbalance between the freedom of single individuals and single social groups has the appearance of order, of institutional justice.

This appearance of justice, that is, the more or less sincere conviction of the majority of individuals to live in a system which, despite all its defects, is substantially just, is precisely the result of the task entrusted to ideologies and propaganda, a task which has the purpose of calming the social body perpetuating at the same time the privileges of those in power because of their accumulation and in view of an even greater accumulation. But every ideological construct, every institutional order, is nothing more than the coulisse of a theatrical performance whose sole purpose is to make the actors feel at ease in their roles, whatever these might have happened to be. Such background scenery, which every historical epoch and every ideology passes off as reality, is however nothing more than a painted flat surface. It is not real. Reality is behind it, beside and all around it. Reality incorporates it but, in fact, just as painted, bidimensional surfaces serving a specific purpose, a specific representation.

Behind the coulisse there is a reality hidden from the actors themselves and shown only if and when necessary: the difference in the degree of violence that can be exercised between those who have power and those who do not. Every inequality of power is based in its essence on the unequal capacity to force other men and women to submit to their will, in the unequal capacity for coercion and to exert on others the violence necessary to subject them, be they individuals, societies or nations, to one's will. Behind the scenes of the established order are the police vans. Behind the ideologies there are the prisons, the fires of the inquisition, the tanks.

Precisely this inequality of power is the result of inequality in accumulation. On the one hand accumulation is in fact already power in itself and it generates power: those who have more than others can always and everywhere afford more than others. This fact, in itself rather banal, is in the end the very motive of accumulation: to increase one's chances of surviving another winter, of not being enslaved but rather to own slaves, of living in ease rather than in need, of being able to lead an existence without worries instead of having to go to work every day. On the other hand, in addition to being power in itself and generating it, accumulation can also buy itself the power it lacks. Indeed, power, a public office, the impunity for a crime or even divine indulgence after death, being rare and desirable, is also a commodity. And, as such, it is also traded, sold by those who can sell it and bought by those who can afford it. As a commodity, however, it is in great demand, since it allows the accumulation itself to be fed even more. Those who pay for power not only buy a consumer good for visibility and prestige, but above all invest their money in the hope of increasing it. Accumulation and power are like two snakes that feed on each other and that, in doing so, grow at the same time: accumulation is, generates and appropriates power, because power is also the guarantee of further accumulation, security, ease, luxury, opulence, madness.

The reason why Plato's republic is destined to remain a philosophical utopia lies in the ingenuity of hypothesizing that there could be a society in which those with the greatest powers have renounced all material possessions. It was the dream of a philosopher who, hoping to educate a tyrant, was eventually sold as a slave. Whenever the social, ideological or hierarchical order between groups and nations is questioned, whoever holds power, today as in the centuries and millennia that preceded us, does not hesitate to use all the necessary violence available to defend their interests. In this specific respect, there is no difference between a gang of street children, large criminal organizations and dictatorships. The international context is not an exception either. One has only to observe how the nations that today enjoy significant military supremacy treat all the others, allies or enemies they might be. When there are differences of power at stake, the use of double moral standards and different parameters of judgment is the rule, not the exception. *Let a prince conquer the state* (i.e. the power) and the means to maintain it will be considered honest and praised. The end, the power, does not justify the means, but it determines them. And it justifies them later, if it really has to, and as far as it can.

In our historical epoch every state claims for it-self the monopoly on exercisable violence and, if this is shown with measure and with the consent of the majority of citizens, it is not because history has become less brutal or superfluous, but because the ideological and institutional mechanisms aimed at securing social consensus still work and avoid the need for physical, head-on confrontation. However, where the power structure is effectively challenged by new forces of comparable strength, ideology and religions, institutions and social order are immediately shaken to the roots and violence explodes in all its brutality, burning whatever it touches in the form of family dramas, gang wars, riots and repressions, coups, revolutions or even world wars.

> The laws made by the governments for their own interests are the justice which they deliver to their subjects and their transgressor is punished as a breaker of the law ... Everywhere justice is only the interest of the stronger.
> (Plato, *The Republic*)

> The dominant thought is always the thought of the dominant class.
> (Karl Marx, *The German Ideology*)

6. The institutional and juridical system, law as a whole, is nothing but the expression of the power relations in force between the various social elements at the moment in which it was established. As such, law is always a snapshot of the past, the

image of the power relations in force at a given historical moment. But these relationships change over time. Individuals or groups increase their power while others lose it. As long as the legal system is an adequate reflection of reality, then *formal law* (formally institutionalized norms) and *factual law*, what happens in everyday life, substantially coincide and it can be said that the rule of law is in force, i.e. that the system of powers that have found expression in the existing juridical system actually reflects the reality.

In addition to formalizing existing power relations and regulating life and social interactions, formal law can also be used as an instrument of control and repression. Where the rules are deliberately vague or simply too many, it is easy to prosecute any journalist, intellectual or political opponent because there will always be some law that he will have unknowingly broken. In modern states, where there are typically well over one hundred thousand laws and regulations that every single citizen should theoretically know and comply with, no one can be sure of respecting all of them and all citizens are, consequently, blackmailable. The fact that those who can often resort to the legal liquidation of their opponents (or of those who simply fall out of their favor) with allegations of any kind and trials under any pretext should not arouse any surprise in those who regularly follow the political news. The current legal system, ideally a protection net against abuses, can in fact very easily become, in the wrong hands, a heinous means of intimidation, persecution and political revenge.

Whenever the formal law, the complex of norms and institutions regulating the functioning of a society, is no longer mirroring the current power relations, it is rendered obsolete and emptied of its meaning by daily practice, that is, by what I just called *factual law*. Whenever major crimes go unpunished and individuals, companies or states, while acting clearly against laws and principles firmly anchored in the law, are not sanctioned in any way, this is a sign that real-life law (similarly to what happens in the *Realpolitik*) is different from the formal one. In fact, it is the existing relations of power that determine what is actually lawful (i.e. feasible) and what is illegal (sanctioned if done). And they always do it first and foremost on the real level. The formal, codified law therefore adapts to the powers' reality if it can and as soon as it can. Ideally this should happen through the regular legislative activity, through the modification of those parts of the constitutions and laws that became obsolete (no longer in line with the current balance of powers) but, where the formal legal system is so obsolete and archaic as to be no longer reformable, such an adjustment can also take place through a sudden outbreak of violence, as in the case of revolutions. Elsewhere, where formal law serves as a fig leaf to cover clearly immoral and unacceptable practices and realities, adaptation may not take place at all, since it is considered more convenient to preach well and scratch badly.

In all cases, however, it is always the real-life law to rule a society, the result of the forces existing within the social body, because whoever has the power to control the wills or at least the behavior of others always makes use of such a power by shaping at will (and in open conflict with other powers, if necessary) the reality of the social order, its ideologies and laws.

7. Accumulation generates poverty. This claim is not as trivial as it might seem at first glance. First of all, because direct interested parties willingly propagate the opposite (and obviously false) idea that the well-being of the wealthier classes spreads downwards in society, which is why it makes sense to reduce taxes for those who are particularly wealthy while maintaining a high tax burden on the other social strata, as in the US-Republican *trickle-*

down economics. According to this theory, the servant must thank heaven for having a master who gives him orders and, goodness of him, something to do during the day. The logical audacity of this reasoning, which we will not dwell on, would have aroused the admiration of the ancient Greek sophists. Its purpose is obviously not the truth, but rather the creation of an evocative scenery to make others believe that what the government is going to do anyway, let the rich pay less tax, has scientific justification. Power justifies its means (we said it already) as well as it can.

But a further, more relevant reason why the assertion that accumulation generates poverty is not trivial is that it carries the curious implication that anyone, any party, government or international institution, who really wants to fight poverty must first and foremost fight the accumulative processes in place since the beginning of history, reversing their trend. From this comes the literally subversive, and therefore rather unlikely, character of a real fight against poverty.

Accumulation generates poverty in two respects. We will discuss the second in a few pages' time. The first, however, is that the accumulation mechanisms just discussed, the subjugation of others and the hoarding of resources, allow the accumulation precisely and only insofar as through them a flow of wealth is generated towards the *owner* (allow me to use this rather generic term), flow that otherwise would not occur. But what can be accumulated is not infinite. The arable land is not infinite, nor are the metals extractable from its depths, nor are the animals we feed on. Whenever someone gets something from the work of others or from the society in which he or she lives, whenever someone appropriates natural resources hitherto available to all, all the others are simultaneously deprived of the exact same amount of wealth.

Thus, if subjugating human beings and making them work for themselves allows the slave master or the owner of a business to enrich himself, it is because through their work, slaves and employees generate a value that is partly taken away from them to go to the master that is enriched by it. If this were not the case, there would be no interest whatsoever in subjugating others, nor in hiring employees. It is only when it is believed that one more employee can generate more profit for the business that an employer hires.

Wherever resources are limited, the transfer of part of them from one individual to another, or from one nation to another, deprives the former of what the latter gets. One euro in my pocket is one euro less for everyone else. It is mine. And if I pass it on to someone else for any reason, he will have one euro more and I will inevitably have one euro less. Through the subjugation of others and the hoarding of resources, he who accumulates deprives the whole community of what he manages to accumulate. Everybody else has become, both in an absolute sense and in relation to him, poorer.

8. From a mere legal point of view, accumulative processes can take place legally, on the basis of formal law, or illegally, on the basis of real-life, factual law. On the individual level, what is illegal falls into the categories of fraud, theft, robbery, extortion etc. On the international level, its equivalent is whatever results from the application of force, such as the occupation of territories, acts of aggression and wars of conquest. Legal, on the other hand, are those mechanisms of accumulation permitted by the formal law and accepted by the current ideology, as slavery was in Greece or Rome (where it was also ethically justified, so as to grant the masters a peaceful sleep) or as dependent work is in today's world.

The most widely used legal form of wealth transfer since the beginning of history, however, the form that has reached an unprecedented level in the present era, is *trade*. The advantage of trade as a method of accumulation is obvious: it is absolutely legal, there is no need to exercise violence, buyer and seller are both satisfied by a voluntary and friendly exchange and, although stigmatized since ancient times, those who practice it today enjoy full social respect. What few buyers consider when they decide to buy, however, is that, with that act of purchase, they surrender part of their wealth to the seller. With the act of purchase, what they have accumulated is reduced by a certain amount, whether small or large, which passes to the seller's nest egg. When this process accelerates rapidly as in the current world, where the purchase is destined for consumption in the short or medium term and an ever greater quantity of goods and services are produced and continuously exchanged, the process of transfer of wealth accelerates and acquires the character of consumerism, which is nothing other than the acceleration of the accumulation processes linked to trade.

To understand why every act of sale is equivalent to a net transfer of wealth from the buyer to the seller, we should start with a simple question: why does every seller want to sell us his product? Certainly not to combat boredom, because there are better alternatives, but not even for the sole desire to recover the costs he incurred, because it would have been more convenient not to have incurred those costs in the first place, rather than assuming them and then trying to recover them. The motive of every seller lies in the prospect of generating, through the act of sale, a profit for himself. Profit is what, once all costs have been subtracted, makes the seller richer than he was before the sale. In the absence of it, the seller would have no reason to exercise his trade. By accepting the agreed price, the buyer voluntarily and implicitly decides to pass part of his wealth on to the seller in exchange for the satisfaction of his legitimate need (or for the fulfillment of his desire).

If we take into account the fact that a product is the result of an entire value chain that goes from the extraction of the raw material to its final form through various stages of transformation, packaging, transport and intermediate sales, it becomes clear that the price of the product in the showcase includes not only the profit of the last seller, the shopkeeper, but also all the profits involved in the intermediate steps of the value chain. The last buyer, with his purchase decision, thus effectively becomes the one who makes all intermediate sellers richer by giving them a part of his wealth, a greater or smaller percentage of the purchase price.

It is only for this reason that trade exists and is encouraged as much as possible, and it is for this reason that the present society has gradually transformed itself into a consumer society, in which as many goods and services as possible must be produced and sold at a constantly increasing speed. The consumer is subjected daily to a psychological bombardment of advertising that has the sole purpose of inducing him to make more and more purchases, so that he surrenders more often and faster minimal parts of his wealth. The introduction of the credit card and of the other cashless and contactless payment methods that followed it spares the buyer the annoying feeling of having to deprive himself of something in exchange for something else. The material act of extracting from his pockets the cash for which he has had to work and of leaving it at the cash desk of the shop is, in fact, avoided. The credit card, a cute and colorful rectangle of plastic (which, moreover, tickles the ego by suggesting a feeling of well-being and financial power), is in fact returned to him intact at the end of the transaction and the painful sight of how much he is actually paying for the product was graciously spared to him. Today's online purchase and payment options allow the consumer to stay sitting in his chair, making sure that without any material payment, without any human interaction and without any physical movement, the object of his desires is discreetly deposited on his doorstep within a matter of hours. All these are the current forms of an increasingly pervasive and pain-free trade for consumption less and less inhibited by physical or psychological barriers. And yet, all the innovations aimed at facilitating the purchase by making it child's play do not change at all the essence of trade: under normal circumstances, that is, wherever everything takes place in a context of freedom and choice (rather than of coercion and necessity), every act of sale represents both an impoverishment of the buyer and an enrichment of the seller. Always.

Who buys gets poorer, who sells richer.

This, and no other, is the soul and the intrinsic motivation of trade, what has caused whole caravans to move at great risk between the East and Europe, that men were captured to be sold as slaves, that entire fleets still face the whims of the sea today or that unimaginable capital is spent every day in marketing and advertising, i.e. in the increasingly aggressive attempt to lure customers for products that are less and less necessary and with an ever shorter life.

It is not from the benevolence of the butcher, the
brewer, or the baker that we expect our dinner,
but from their regard to their own interest.
(Adam Smith, *An Inquiry into the Nature and
Causes of the Wealth of Nations*)

An entire historical epoch, that of mercantilism
or mercantile capitalism, was founded at the end of
the Middle Ages on an unprecedented expansion of
trade, both locally and, even more so, internation-
ally. Between the sixteenth and eighteenth centuries the merchants acquired an influence and
power within the social body that they had never
had in the predominantly agricultural societies of
antiquity and the Middle Ages. They actually ruled
the richest cities, from Venice to Florence, from
Bruges to London, and even played a decisive role
in the birth and development of national states,
seen as mere instruments and guarantors of their
own interests, in essence, of the accumulation of
their profits. A notable effect brought about by the
mercantile revolution was also a cultural change:
personal enrichment ceased to be ethically questioned or condemned by theologians. Getting rich
in every legally possible way became ethically acceptable, socially advantageous and a clear sign of

wit and intelligence if not, indeed, of heavenly blessing.

The profit generated by trade, that is, from every single act of sale, becomes part of the savings, of the assets, of the seller. And it is precisely the increase in what is individually owned that constitutes that accumulation process that has moved history since its origins. Measurable in sacks of grain, in gold or in currency, this increase is the motive of the trader, how much he manages to subtract from the buyer in ways (mostly, but not always) that are completely legal and accepted by custom. Every deed of sale, apparently a mere exchange of goods, is always in fact and above all an unequal exchange of value, a net passage of wealth from the buyer to the seller. In exchange for his own impoverishment, the buyer has obtained a service, a good or a commodity that he can consume and enjoy, or which he can try to use to generate value on its turn (investment).

But what exactly is *value*?

9. The real value of a good or service is the price a buyer would be willing to pay for it in the moment the good is put on sale or the service is offered. It is the market value of the good or service in question at a given time. Being based on an exchange, the

value attributable to something is actually measured in terms of a second commodity (usually currency) which, a commodity itself, is also subject to fluctuations in value.

An interesting consequence of this fact is that, in an isolated economic system, without exchanges with the outside world, the value remains constant: every individual of such a system, like every society or every nation in it, has in fact always and only a limited amount of savings that he can use at will. The finitude of his savings forces each subject to make a continuous choice about how to use the value at his disposal, and it is evident that, if for any reason the value attributed to a specific commodity increases, the value attributed by the subject to another commodity or service has to decrease at the same time. In other words, for each single buyer the total value of the products on the market is actually the total value of his savings. An increase in the number of products on the market allows for a wider choice, but does not imply a corresponding increase in their overall value, which is instead linked to the total value of the savings available in the system in question.

In an isolated economic system, regardless of the quantity of goods and services offered, regardless of the fact that new products are placed on the market every day, their overall value is therefore destined to remain constant over time. Consequently, as supply increases, everything constantly depreciates, and if it does not seem so, because perhaps the prices remain the same while goods and services increase in quantity, it is only because the money itself used in the exchange loses value at the same time, so that it is not a surprise that in terms of value with a euro today one gets much less than what one could get for it twenty years ago and that, in general, one has the impression that everything is getting more and more expensive.

Such a de-*valuation* (not necessarily equivalent to a de-*preciation*) tends to affect every commodity on the market: material goods, services, but also educational qualifications for example or, indeed, the currency itself. A consequence of the constancy of the total value present in an isolated economic system and of the simultaneous increase in the goods (in a broad sense) available on the market, the devaluation of individual goods is aggravated and accelerated by a further factor: we do not live in an economically isolated system at all.

If our economic system, considered on a planetary scale, were in fact an isolated system, the principle of the constancy of the total value would have as a paradoxical consequence the fact that the whole of humanity today would not be a cent richer than the few thousand hominids that in prehistoric times lived in caves and dressed in skins. But, as in the case of the principle of conservation of energy, that of conservation of the overall economic value must take into account the fact that the earth, and with it the economic system of the whole of humanity, are not closed systems. Just as the earth receives energy from the sun every day, and in fact exactly for the same reason (the life that the light and the heat of the sun allow on earth), our economic system also increases its resources over time. Economic resources, that is, those endowed with a value, are all by definition limited and desirable, but can also be divided into renewable or non-renewable. The former, such as the products of the land and the sea or renewable energies in general, if well managed can be used and regenerated, but they are usually also perishable: they should be consumed immediately, in the short or at most in the medium term. Their value depends on their availability and momentary desirability. The latter, such as fossil fuels, are characterized by the fact that their availability decreases with their use. Their value increases with their scarcity, which tends to be ever increasing, and with their desirability.

In terms of value, non-renewable resources do not inject any into the economic system. They have always been there, so to speak, and can only be used or not. But renewable resources, if properly used, increase what is available to humanity constantly and free of charge, for example in terms of agricultural products or electricity.

A particularly important factor in the creation of value starting from available resources is also assumed by human and animal work in general. If every day millions of new artifacts are added to what is already available on the market it is because every day the work of man produces them ceaselessly, and this since the dawn of time. The production of land and seas creates value because, through work, it constantly offers man, communities and whole nations new materials and products to be exchanged and, thus, additional value. Therefore, if we are not as poor as our distant prehistoric ancestors it is because we were lucky enough to be born after many thousands of years of harvesting, fishing and hard work. It seems paradoxical that the possibility we have of creating value every day can contribute to a constant devaluation of everything that is offered on the market, including money, but it is so. And it is so because the continuous creation of value that land and work allow always translates into a greater abundance of goods and services, which are therefore subject to constant average devaluation. Only what remains or becomes increasingly rare continues to maintain or even manages to increase its value. This is the case, for example, for non-renewable resources, for estates in the historic centers of some cities, for unique works of art or for rarities for collectors. And this happens according to the law of supply and demand. To increase its value, however, what is or becomes rare must also remain desirable and not easily replaceable: the last barrel of oil will either have an exorbitant price tag or will lie unsold in the general disinterest.

Thus, if on the one hand renewable resources allow a constant increase in the overall value existing in our economic system, on the other hand this continuously increasing availability causes a devaluation of every single commodity. The result of the interaction of these two factors in terms of prices will therefore depend on the variations over time in the supply and demand of the individual commodities, including money. Such fluctuations, by determining their mutual values, will cause the price of certain commodities to rise and that of others to fall.

This excursus allows us to return now to the question of the interdependence of poverty and accumulation. Given that the overall value existing in our economic system, despite all the limits mentioned here, continues to grow due to the generation of new resources and to human work, is it in fact still possible to state that accumulation causes poverty? And, if so, in what sense? A first reason, linked to the exclusivity of the possession of value, has already been discussed. But an even more serious cause of poverty lies in the very nature of accumulative processes, that is, in the circumstance by which those people, entities or nations that already have more also have a greater chance of achieving more in the present and in the future. Because of the economic, social and political power that derives from existing accumulation and because of the social order that reflects and respects the existing power relations, those who have the most attract the available wealth with greater force than other social or international actors can do.

To the extent that the accumulation of value allows those who benefit from it to secure even more value in the future, if not counterbalanced by other factors, it will attract more and more value just as a black hole attracts more and more mass, with the result of draining the sources of value available for other individuals in a community or for other nations in the international context. The power (in the broad sense of the term) always associated with accumulation can in fact be so strong as to ensure that the value that is created daily through natural resources and work flows predominantly towards itself, reducing the economic base of those who remain untouched by this flow.

82% of all growth in global wealth in the last year went to the top 1%.
(Oxfam, *Reward Work, Not Wealth*, 2018)

10. Accumulation grows like a tumor and, in the absence of decisive and adequate (i.e. strong and serious) corrective systems, the gap between wealth and poverty is destined to increase always and everywhere and, moreover, to constantly accelerate in its own dynamics. Needless to say, this process is further aggravated by the constant increase of the world population, a phenomenon whereby the value not yet swallowed up by the top of the society has to be divided, generation after generation, among more and more individuals. To a different extent from one historical epoch to another, to a

different extent from nation to nation, therefore, the ongoing process of accumulation always leads (on average) to a more or less rapid impoverishment of all the other members of the social group.

Accumulation and poverty are thus two sides of the same coin, two phenomena that proceed and amplify mutually. And if this seems contrary to reality, for example because society as a whole seems to get richer and increase its well-being, this happens not because everyone can actually become richer at the same time, but because the well-being of the lucky ones is actually paid for by others. Indeed, there are historical circumstances in which an entire nation seems to flourish and enrich itself, thus enjoying a period of abundance and grace, so to speak, from which a large part of its citizens profit. Italy experienced its golden age with the Renaissance, at the end of the Middle Ages, nations like France, Holland or Great Britain flourished in the following three centuries. The twentieth century was then the US American century, while the one we are living in now seems to be the century of China ... Such happy periods are made possible by historical circumstances that allow a net and huge flow of wealth towards the nations in question.

And, as it happens on the individual level, so also on the international level every transfer of value is always linked to forms that can be legally acceptable, such as international trade or the transfer of industries and production to low-cost countries, or to forms characterized from more or less implicit recourse to coercion and violence, corruption, occupation, aggression, enslavement, destabilization. Either way, however, the well-being of the nations privileged by a certain historical conjuncture is always paid for by other nations and other peoples in terms of individual and collective exploitation or, simply, of gradual impoverishment. Before our eyes, still today nations endowed with great natural wealth, especially in Africa and the Middle East, are maintained or constantly plunged into a state of crisis and dependence for the sole purpose of being able to loot them for the strategic interests of the dominant nations, oftentimes with the help of corrupt local governments kept alive and in power by the dollars and the weapons of their actual and invisible masters.

When the wealth that a nation manages to attract is no longer sufficient to guarantee the well-being of society as a whole, or when the entire social body is impoverished, the golden period, the economic boom, ends and decline starts: the whole society falls ill. Just as a body is healthy when all its parts and organs are in a functional balance, so a society is healthy as long as all its components are in a reciprocal functional balance in which no part is overstrained by the needs of another. A community of people is stable and functional as long as all its members feel adequately represented and free in it and as long as individuals have the feeling that they are partaking of the well-being dividends in economic, social and political terms.

In the absence of external sources of wealth, however, the ongoing accumulative processes increase social differences and erode the social balance on several fronts. When the differences of wealth, and therefore of power, tear the social fabric giving rise to disparities, abuses that go unpunished or evident injustices, the social body is dismembered and particular interests overcome the general sense of solidarity. Repressed protests, civil unrest or mass migration follow. Or it may happen that the entire state apparatus, apparently still every day at their workplace, simply stops working because no one believes anymore in the meaningfulness of what should be done. In the worst case, the erosion of the social fabric can result in brutal repression, coups d'état supported by poorly paid militias or outright revolutions that quickly wipe out decades-old, if not even centuries-old, regimes.

It is the accumulation itself that generates this dangerous social decay. This, in fact, is caused by the increase in poverty and in inequality induced by the accumulative processes in the social body, by the difference in terms of political power (and impunity) that excessive accumulation ends up creating between the corrupt ruling elite and the great majority of people who have the sole task of working and staying calm to keep the system running.

The progressive social erosion caused by accumulation is due to the economic unsustainability of the accumulation process itself. The continuous transfer of value from those who have less to those who have more, if not corrected, is doomed to destroy the social consensus and, with this, itself. If such an event, predicted by Karl Marx in the nineteenth century, has not yet occurred in the terms imagined at that time, it is because the industrialized societies on which Marx had based his analysis have found a way to guarantee a minimum of collective growth at the expense of others, nations and populations who have become external victims of this growth. The progressive impoverishment of the masses foreseen in industrialized societies was in fact avoided only thanks to the expansion made possible by colonialism first and by imperialism thereafter – a military imperialism that became, in the second half of the twentieth century and after two world wars disastrous for Europe, postcolonial imperialism and financial subjugation of countries in Africa, Asia and Latin America. The cost of the reconstruction and development of Western well-being, as well as of the industrialized world in general, is in fact paid only in part by the classes of these countries. The rest is sustained and suffered by the populations of other continents, enslaved militarily and economically by stronger nations.

This form of externalization of the costs of accumulation, however, cannot continue indefinitely. The rampant poverty in many countries of the world today destabilizes those countries, and at the same time has set in motion, since the end of the nineteenth century, a migratory movement of epoch-making dimensions and destined to increase in the future. The indecency of the physical, military and bureaucratic walls in which Europe or the United States are increasingly closing in to stem the arrival of the men, women and children that the richer regions have reduced to poverty is doomed to failure (besides being shaming) because there are no walls high enough or long enough to stop a process destined to definitively change the course of human history. But the walls are also of little use in a second sense: that the globalization of production and markets that capitalist development has sought and generated in an attempt to save itself from its own economic consequences has produced poverty within the very countries that seek to protect themselves from migratory movements.

The epidemic is already within the city walls.

The transfer of production to low-cost countries, the prime mover of globalization always in search of the minimization of costs for the maximization of profit, also entails a reduction in savings (and therefore an impoverishment) in those countries where production, i.e. work itself, the source of income, is lost. In ancient times and in the Middle Ages those who owned large estates, servants and slaves were enriched directly by what came from these resources and based their lifestyle on the certainty of such a constant influx of wealth. In today's world, however, those who get rich thanks to the work carried out in low-cost countries by workers and employees in a state of semi-slavery are not those to whom the products are destined, but rather the industries and corporations to which capital and production belong. The citizens of wealthier countries and with a more lavish lifestyle, once deprived of the possibility of enriching themselves through their work, now too expensive for the producers, are so reduced to mere consumers to be lured with increasingly attractive offers and apparently indispensable products. The thousand-year-old economic dyad

servant – master

has thus become the triad

(low-cost) worker – corporation – consumer

in which the latter serves only, as long as he still has savings, to finance the profits of the corporation and is seen by this as a simple cash cow, a lemon to be squeezed. In the course of this wondrous transmutation, the ideal citizen has become a quiet consumer. He still works, if he can, but above all he consumes, pays taxes, keeps himself healthy, but has the decency not to live too long so as not to aggravate the budgets of the pension systems. He votes for respectable parties, he does not save excessively and, what he saves, he entrusts to the banks so that they can make their profit out of it. He is too busy with his work or his consumption to reflect on the system in which he lives and to question it. He has to eat, drink and have fun (*bread and circuses*), he is not so poor that he cannot spend, nor so rich as to become a threat to those who are really rich. He respects the laws and the authorities, and sacrifices private interest to what he is told is the public interest. He believes in politicians who look serious, does not lean towards heresies and remains reasonable and reasonably calm. The citizen-consumer is not only harmless to the system of accumulation but is also useful to it. He is isolated, can be eliminated and can be black-mailed if necessary. He is obedient and traceable, since he is not opposed either to the control of his movements, his communications and his economic transactions, or to the commercialization of his personal data or his dietary, cultural or sexual pref-erences. The erosion of the private sphere and the commodification of his entire existence do not bother him.

In essence, however, the peaceful citizens and consumers of today's industrialized countries live off the value accumulated over the past centuries. Their consumption is made possible by what they already have, not by how much in terms of new wealth they still manage to accumulate. Following the production and sale of goods and services like a shadow, value has in fact been moving for decades to outside the industrialized Western world, espe-cially towards Asia and, more particularly, towards China.

Moreover, globalization has made national economies largely anachronistic and irrelevant and has had the result of making the whole world a single economy in which an increasingly small group of privileged people (individuals or industries) faces a large mass of dispossessed people and a middle class that, everywhere, struggles not to be sucked into poverty by savings that are gradually dwindling. With the globalization of the economy, contrary to what happened in the nineteenth and twentieth centuries, no outsourcing is possible anymore: there are no longer others who can pay the costs of our well-being or, to use a catchphrase, *we* are now the *others*. Once a planetary-scale economy is reached, there cannot be any further expansion of the markets. And this has, in long-standing industrialized countries, heavy social and political repercussions.

A failure to resolve the root causes of economic inequality and specifically social mobility will inevitably lead to sustained civil unrest.
(Atelier BNP Paribas, *A Promise Broken*, 2022)

11. The political system in any given nation can reveal a lot about what happens in that country in

terms of accumulation. Indeed, different political regimes correspond, as effects and symptoms, to different stages of the accumulative processes.

From the point of view of accumulation, absolutist and illiberal systems offer as a matter of fact the greatest potential for an extremely wealthy oligarchy to rule over a multitude of people who pay the costs of such a regime in terms of suffering and misery. On the other side of this spectrum are liberal democracies: together with a maximum of individual freedoms, they also involve a wide distribution of powers which, when functioning, curbs accumulative excesses and social differences between citizens.

In cumulative terms, therefore, democracy is expensive. It is in a certain sense a luxury, a political regime that presupposes a minimum of equality and the distribution of power and wealth. Its processes, its institutions, a functioning system without making corruption necessary for every single employee and the diversion of funds essential for every politician, as well as the freedom of choice and life of every single citizen, have in fact a considerable influence on the quality and on the speed of accumulation, a much higher influence than what happens in all those regimes which, without having to compromise socially, rely on the brutality of their security apparatuses.

A functioning democracy represents a state of grace of society, a state of historical balance which, however, like every balance, can also be lost when one of the forces that contribute to the status quo consistently becomes more intense than those that counter it. In a world where wealth continues to concentrate itself in fewer and fewer hands, where public budgets and services must be cut and living standards are deteriorating, it is therefore no surprise to see that so many democracies are becoming less and less liberal and that populism, nationalism and autocracies are progressing everywhere, even in those countries that have been the cradle and touchstone of democracy.

The deterioration of democracy and its institutions is not a direct effect of cuts to budgets or services, but rather of the deterioration of the social fabric which is the foundation of democracy itself, which is the nourishment of its institutions. And this is a direct effect of accumulation. Where citizens slip into poverty or live in a state that is less and less capable of guaranteeing essential services, their impatience is directed straight towards politics and they become critical of the institutions. Social solidarity, the idea of collectivity itself and the community of objectives and destinies falter and centrifugal forces, as well as a general *every man for himself!* panic, spread like a fire that burns trust and optimism and with them the democratic institutions themselves.

Societies in which the gap between a few rich and many more or less poor increases, a society in which individuals must continually cut their expenses and in which the state must continually borrow and decrease the quality of the services offered, are sick societies, societies in which the feeling of belonging and the trust in democracy are slowly but surely running out. In this sense, the distribution of wealth within the social body is also an index, albeit a coarse one, of the state of health of the society in question. In fact, it offers a snapshot of the momentary arrival point of the accumulation process and of the level of damage already caused within the social body.

Moreover, with the forced passage of accumulative processes from a national level (as it still was a century ago) to globalization, the nation states, at their birth temple of the interests of the rich and trading classes, have definitively lost control of the economic processes that take place in them. They have lost power. They themselves have become less significant, if not at times completely irrelevant, because commerce, in its race for accumulation and profit, has left them behind, making them institutional vestiges of the past, guardians of an empty room.

The social, economic and institutional degeneration that Western democracies have to face today also affects, albeit to a different extent, every other regime, forced more and more to resort to force to lower the costs imposed by individual freedom and to keep themselves in power in a world which, now globalized, becomes more and more unequal, populated and poor.

Those who have so far taken advantage of accumulation and hold power are trying everywhere and by all means to prevent their social environment from entering the magmatic stage in which everything is questioned and political and economic outcomes are uncertain and ungovernable. Such a concordance of interests of the ruling classes to justify and maintain the status quo by all means has, of course, always existed. It has always constituted that system of power in which individuals are born, grow up and are educated and indoctrinated. It is a system that has and always has had a hundred names: god, king, country, pope and faith, master or lord, president, Your Highness, order, well-being ... but as the accumulative processes proceed, we always arrive at a historical point in which the divergence between the public narrative of the system, its founding dogma, collides with the daily reality experienced by each individual. Just as no plan survives first contact with the enemy (Helmuth von Moltke), no dogma resists impact with reality. The collision between an obsolete social order and reality is a moment marked by the evident overcoming of formal law and the perceived sense of social justice. *Factual law* comes out clearly in the open: large and small crimes go unpunished, corruption and the arrogance of power, together with its obvious inability to guarantee a decent life to one's fellow citizens, poison society. When this happens the institutions go into necrosis, the social body, by now irremediably ill, enters a stage whose outcome can only be either a slow, continuous degradation or a new social order. It is never a painless situation, as it costs lives, suffering and enormous economic resources which those in power try by any means to manage or avoid, if necessary even by force and with the most brutal of repressions.

Thus, while on the one hand democracies undergo an involution and an illiberal, populist and anachronistically nationalistic drift that corrodes their credibility and institutions, on the other hand the authoritarian states become more and more brutal and repressive while still others fall into the hands of shabby, but no less dangerous, military juntas. Finally, the last ones, the most miserable and desperate of the states, continue to exist only on the world map and in hypocritical diplomatic speeches, but have in fact ceased to exist to become territories without borders, ruled by warlords and local militias without any future prospects.

> Many present efforts to guard and maintain
> human progress, to meet human needs, and to
> realize human ambitions are simply unsustainable
> – in both the rich and poor nations ... They may
> show profit on the balance sheets of our
> generation, but our children will inherit the losses.
> (*Brundtland Report*, 1987)

12. Based on the form predominantly assumed, four major historical phases of the accumulation process can be distinguished: the era of land accumulation, based on the acquisition of lands, servants and slaves as labor force, lasting from the antiquity until the Middle Ages, the epoch of mercantile accumulation, based on the expansion of trade between the sixteenth and eighteenth centuries, the

capitalist phase of accumulation, based on industrial production, colonialism and imperialism and lasting until the Second World War, and, finally, the time of consumerist accumulation, based on an unprecedented supply of consumer goods, products and services made possible by a dense global production and logistics network, as well as by the advent of informatics and the internet. Common to all these forms of accumulation has been and remains the simultaneous exploitation of all that the planet has to offer in terms of resources. As far as this point is concerned, however, a notable change has occurred in the last three hundred years.

As long as man cultivated and harvested the fruit of his work in the fields, as long as he moderately hunted, fished or extracted minerals from the earth, his environmental impact was limited to the reduction of wildlife on earth and the accumulation always remained substantially sustainable: the planetary ecosystem was never seriously threatened by human activities. Over the last few centuries, however, the ecologically sustainable accumulation, substantially based on the use of resources that the earth was able to regenerate, has been gradually replaced by an accumulation based on an intensive exploitation of non-renewable resources, starting with the fossil fuels needed to power industrial production and to cover the demand for energy arising for instance from household, work or transport needs.

This passage, which roughly coincides with the industrial revolution, has had the effect of improving human living conditions to the point of triggering an unprecedented demographic development. In the last three centuries the world population has thus jumped from the approximately 500 million previously (and very slowly) reached to nearly eight billion today. In turn, such demographic expansion has had an impact on the planet in terms of resources, as it requires more land, more food, more energy, more urban spaces and a multitude of industrial products.

With this step, the ecological unsustainability of accumulation has transcended the simple use of non-renewable resources, has gone beyond the use of fossil fuels, and has begun to affect the very capability of the earth to regenerate those resources which, in principle, had always been renewable. With the increase in population and with the growth of industrial needs, as well as accumulative processes, the relationship between man and the earth has definitively changed and the ecosystem in which we all live today is now threatened by four factors that attack the planet at the same time:

• the consumption of non-renewable resources which, without an adequate technological leap, will lead to their exhaustion with dramatic consequences,

• the reduction and degradation of sustainable resources, biodiversity and natural spaces, with direct consequences on ecosystems and therefore on life on earth itself,

• the pollution caused both by industrial production and by our needs and lifestyles, which has a direct impact on the quality of air and water, as well as on the arable land, its products and our own health,

• and, finally, the climate change which, with the rise of average temperatures, leads to a destabilization of the climatic and environmental balance already observable today.

These factors lead to an environmental degradation which, in economic terms, translates into costs – rising costs to cover energy needs and the consequences of climate change, rising costs to cover the nutritional needs of a growing population at a time when the seas have less fish to offer and few areas can be added to the stock of arable lands. If these costs are not paid directly by individuals, they are mostly paid by the states (therefore once again by the community), but they are also felt in social terms, with entire sections of the world's population condemned to live in degraded environmental conditions, in which the quality of food, water and air threaten the health and the survival of entire communities.

Furthermore, accumulative processes increase the divergence between wealth and poverty also under the environmental aspect. It is not the rich or the affluent who have to live in degraded and polluted homes and urban environments. They are not the ones who have to feed on industrial products that are harmful to their health, nor who have to drink contaminated water or have to breathe poisoned air. Those who have adequate economic resources do not have to face the prospect of working in unhealthy environments, nor do they risk having to migrate to survive or having a shorter life expectancy. The need to scavenge through garbage to find something to resell is unknown to them, the very idea absurd. On the contrary, those who have had the luck to be born in a situation of relative financial stability have no reason to exercise any restraint or any renunciation – they are privileged.

But it is always a privilege that is paid for by the lives deprived, if not actually led in misery, of the other, less fortunate inhabitants of the earth, the majority.

The affluent part of mankind can not only still afford to live according to its wishes, but contributes with its lifestyle more than anybody else to the environmental degradation of the planet. The accounts of such existential tranquility are settled in other parts of the city and in other countries of the world, where environmental degradation and the scarcity of resources are causes of instability, insecurity, crime, migration and conflicts.

Ensuring access to essential resources in an international framework in which these resources, limited by nature, are decreasing more and more engages all states in a struggle pursued without scruples and by every means (political, financial, military) for access to water, land, fuels and minerals required to ensure social stability, industrial production and military superiority. It is an underground conflict, less evident than an open war (to which it does lead sometimes), but no less relevant, a conflict in which the most powerful states play their geopolitical dominance and the lesser ones fight for their survival.

And yet, the ecological effect of accumulative processes is potentially catastrophic for the whole of life on earth. Production, consumption, appropriation and exploitation find their physical and insurmountable limit in the finitude and fragility of the planet on which we all have the common destiny to live. The resources that our lifestyle requires day after day and the damage that, day after day, our form of civilization causes in terms of pollution and destruction, if not addressed and stopped in time, are a threat to the very survival of humanity on the planet.

Southern trees bear a strange fruit
Blood on the leaves and blood at the root.
(Abel Meeropol, *Strange Fruit*)

Here and Now

The processes described so far have taken place over centuries, if not millennia. Where are we today?

1. Regarding the distribution of wealth, a few pieces of data can provide a good overview: in individual terms, one percent of the world population owns more than half of the world's wealth, while only eight men own as much as the poorest half of the world.[1] At corporate level, a study based on data from 2007 concluded that 147 transnational corporations own 40% of the total value of all transnational corporations combined while, at the regional level, North America and Europe is home to more than 60% of the world's wealth, the rest being divided among the remaining continents (including

---

[1] Oxfam, *An Economy for the 99%*, 2017. Credit Suisse, by means of its *wealth pyramid*, analyses the distribution of wealth with similar results.

Africa, which, despite its immense natural resources, has to resign itself to about one percent of global wealth).[2]

These numbers and estimates may fluctuate over time, as well as according to the methods and the sources used in their analysis, but the substance and, above all, their general tendency do not change: the distribution of wealth is strongly unbalanced within the individual countries, among different countries and among the various regions of the world. The imbalance is reflected both on the industrial and on the individual level, where about

---

[2] See Stefania Vitali, James B. Glattfelder, Stefano Battiston, *The Network of Global Corporate Control*, as well as James B. Davies, Susanna Sandström, Anthony F. Shorrocks and Edward N. Wolff, *The Global Distribution of Household Wealth*, UN University – WIDER. Extremely interesting in this regard is also *The Looting Machine*, a text dedicated to the pillage of the African continent by Tom Burgis, correspondent for the *Financial Times*. From his introduction: "I started to see the thread that connects a massacre in a remote African village with the pleasures and comforts that we in the richer parts of the world enjoy. It weaves through the globalized economy, from war zones to the pinnacles of power and wealth in New York, Hong Kong and London."

70 million people own as much as the remaining seven and more billion human beings.

Such a concentration of wealth might be expected to correspond to extreme poverty in the rest of the world, but the situation is more complex. The proportion of the world population forced to live below the absolute poverty line (1.90 dollars per day in 2011, according to the definition of the World Bank) has not in fact increased in recent decades but rather, if we exclude sub-Saharan Africa, has in fact decreased.[3] Even relative poverty, although not recording a decrease as sharp as the one shown by absolute poverty, in general has not increased.[4] If the reduction of the most extreme poverty is certainly a fact to rejoice in, one wonders who is paying the bill for accelerating accumulation and diminishing poverty. The answer is twofold: from the individual point of view, in a world with a growing population, in which the wealthiest have more and more and the less well-off are finally able to leave absolute poverty, it can only be the middle (or lower-middle) class who has to settle the bill, that more or less large segment of the population which, even

[3] Various studies agree on this point. See for example USAID, *Getting to Zero*, 2013.

[4] This is the conclusion, for example, of the World Bank in *Poverty and Shared Prosperity 2018: Piecing Together the Poverty Puzzle*.

without being able to define themselves as rich, had achieved a social and financial situation of relative security. From the social point of view, it has often been the state who has settled the bills and the costs of the welfare of its citizens. It has done so, particularly since the 1970s, through state debt. A debt that has never stopped growing since then.

2. Public debt has reached an unprecedented level today, so much so that the mere idea that it will be repaid one day is ridiculous.[5] On the contrary, heavily indebted states are already being tested by the annual payment of interest on their debts alone, which allows their creditors to enjoy an almost eternal and relatively secure income.

The fact that industrialized states and advanced economies have the highest debts (the United States alone holds about a third of the world's public debt) is a clear indication that debt is being used as an economic, political and social stabilization tool. Contracted for the purpose of being able to continue living beyond one's means without major social earthquakes, it has however a high cost and serious consequences. On the one hand, the need to repay it or to minimize further debts leads to a re-

---

[5] The International Monetary Fund estimated it at around 87 trillion dollars in December 2021.

duction in the state budget and all that it entails, with negative repercussions on the state of essential infrastructures, education, work, health, social policies, justice or defense. On the other hand, the debt subdues the state to its creditors, making it incapable of autonomous policy and potential prey to speculative financial maneuvers: debt enslaves. It also costs, and is paid for in terms of economic and political blackmail, and constitutes an actual limitation of national sovereignty.

What, in all this, citizens earn in terms of avoided poverty, they therefore lose in collective terms, having to work a substantial part of the year to generate that tribute which, once destined to the pharaoh, the Roman emperor or the local monastery, is today devolved with slavish gratitude to the creditors of their state, and having to live in a state that is publicly bleeding to death to avoid a social revolt. Thus we move around in everyday life complaining about a state of things that deteriorates from decade to decade, but without really addressing the root of the problem, that is, the collective impoverishment caused by accumulative processes.

A classic example of the procrastination of debt problems and demographic changes in Western societies is represented by the pension system. Retirement pensions, together with all the social safety nets that a state has made available to reduce the economic hardship of its citizens, represent the most important part of the state budget, and therefore also the main cause of the debts incurred by it. With a population getting older and without enough jobs to pay pension entitlements, pension systems have become one of the largest sources of public debt, bottomless sinks that require structural intervention to become more or less controllable. Unfortunately these are interventions that, in a democracy, very few politicians dare to propose, because this would catapult them into opposition at the first opportunity. The result is that the adjustments made to the pension systems remain timid and that, without the contraction of further debts, the risk of a future collapse of the system with entire generations destined for an old age in poverty becomes more and more concrete. The choice between procrastination and debts is not exciting and this is perhaps why states ultimately rely on both options: they postpone the hard necessary reforms as much as they can and borrow as much as they have to.

Where states have tried to avoid the debt trap, it is the population that has been left in the poverty that our model of development, which is intrinsically based on private accumulation, entails. The result of all this is that the middle classes, the backbone of society, either become impoverished and become indebted personally,[6] wherever the state is unwilling to fill the gaps that open up in the system, or they do so collectively, bearing the costs of welfare in the form of public debt and paying them in terms of worsening of services and, therefore, of the quality of life. There actually is an alternative to this state of affairs but, who knows why, it does not seem attractive to those who have the duty to indicate and implement it: a tax system based on assets, rather than on income. We will come back to this point in *due course* (no pun intended).

The level of democracy enjoyed by the average global citizen in 2020 is down to the levels around 1990 ... This reflects an accelerating wave of autocratization.
(V-Dem Institute,
Autocratization Turns Viral, 2021)

---

[6] In addition to approximately 87 trillion dollars of public debt, the International Monetary Fund mentions around 139 trillion dollars of private debt, a historical record as well.

3. Only a minority of men live and exercise their civil and political rights in full freedom. This is about fifteen, perhaps twenty percent of the world population. The rest is divided more or less equally between authoritarian and persecutory regimes, and regimes in which personal freedom and rights are only enjoyable to a limited extent. This already unfortunate situation is aggravated by the fact that liberal democracies have been in slow but steady retreat over the past two decades. Autocracies seem to be advancing everywhere.[7]

Moreover, the decline (or erosion) of democratic values seems to always follow the same script. It begins with the imposition of strict control over the media, civil society and independent intellectual and political groups, then it continues with a mixture of propaganda and the delegitimization of existing democratic institutions and processes to finally impose its own interests and political agenda.

---

[7] It is therefore no coincidence that the latest report from the V-Dem Institute is titled *Autocratization Turns Viral*, while the contemporary report from Freedom House is titled *Democracy under Siege*. The latter reads: "The impact of the long-term democratic decline has become increasingly global in nature, broad enough to be felt by those living under the cruelest dictatorships, as well as by citizens of long-standing democracies."

Exemplified and dramatically staged in the United States during and even more so at the end of the Trump presidency, this decay of political and civil values is a phenomenon that began a long time ago and is much more widespread geographically than one might think at first sight.

In fact, its roots lie in the economic and social crises of the seventies and eighties, due to the shrinking of available resources and opportunities, which resulted in dissatisfaction or suffering of the middle and lower classes. Those unresolved crises, combined with an increased demand for freedom and economic, social and political rights advanced above all by the younger generations, led to an authoritarian reaction that can be recorded both in long-standing democracies and in those regimes that already were authoritarian and despotic.

Those leaders who more than others personify the weakening of institutions, and who take advantage of it for their own concrete personal interests, are not the causes of this decline, but rather its symptoms, its products and effects, the inedible fruits of a sick tree. Their power is made possible by the entire patronage class that they nourish and corrupt with their power, while a good rest of the population, incapable of critical and autonomous political thought, tired of the social involution witnessed in recent decades, fascinated by the mixture of hedonism and impunity that such leaders of decadence emanate, vote for them out of anger, exhaustion, ignorance or even with messianic illusions.

In such socially poisoned climates, even in the wealthiest countries, extreme fringes of the political spectrum, especially those of an anti-system, xenophobic and anti-Semitic right, have grown in terms of political consensus and representation. Liberal societies show serious fault lines between those who in some way still support the national political system out of personal interest or conviction and those who are excluded, marginalized and instigated against the system by the system itself.

On top of this toxic conflict, internal to liberal democracies, there is everywhere in the world a growing conflict at local and regional level due to the decrease of resources and the nullification of opportunities for social mobility. Wherever this happens, wherever power shows a chronic inability to meet the needs of citizens, it falls prey to the fear of being dethroned and increases control over everything it considers hostile: freedom of the press and of expression, journalists and writers, political parties, opposition, peacefully demonstrating citizens. In the delirium of illiberal regimes, everything is suspicion, betrayal, incitement, terrorism.

Thus, while long-standing democracies of great tradition are being eroded from within, the situation in the rest of the world is not the best either and shows no signs of any real social progress. The Islamic world is slowly consumed in the feud between Saudi Arabia, Iran and their respective allies and vassals, a continuous fight dragging one country after another into ruin, from Syria to Yemen, from Libya to Iraq ... Ruled mostly by autocrats courted by the West or by mercenary bands, it has been sliding for decades towards an increasingly gloomy, extreme and intolerant vision of the world of which women and younger generations without decent work and political rights are the main victims. Latin America is in the throes of widespread corruption as well as criminal violence as heinous as it is free to act and rule entire territories at will. Sub-Saharan Africa is devastated by military coups and a worrying inability to guarantee internal security against gangs and militias subsidized by international actors or simply in disarray, while a large part of the continent, where it is not prey to corruption and robbery, remains poor and ungovernable. In Asia, large and small nations (China, Russia, India, but also Afghanistan or Myanmar) are increasingly becoming either illiberal democracies or violent dictatorships.

On all continents ethnic, religious or political intolerance, an expression of misery, conflict and ignorance, is advancing and is skillfully exploited by those, often the highest offices of the state, which can reap significant personal benefits from it and from the fears of ordinary people. The public interest, the spirit of duty, the sense of belonging to the same and unique society, the idea of having a common destiny and future, is slowly abandoning everyone, even those middle classes that represent the most intimate and strong part of the state.

More egalitarian societies, with less extreme differences between their citizens, societies that offer more freedom and justice, are also the least confrontational and the more affluent societies, where everybody would like to and could live with dignity and satisfaction. By orienting ourselves to these values, we would all benefit from them and not just a small minority of privileged people who are dragging their fellow citizens and the whole world to ruin. In the future as the accumulative processes advance, will see an increasingly accentuated contrast between the societies in which the equality of citizens predominates, and which therefore enjoy an enviable collective well-being, even if not excessive, and the societies in which an absolute minority of rich and powerful families despotically rules over controlled and impoverished masses. It is up to all of us to choose which group our society can or should belong to and it is up to us to make this happen. Those who do not claim their rights will be deprived of them.

> War is just the continuation of politics
> by other means.
> (Carl von Clausewitz, *On War*)

4. Since the beginning of history, war has been viewed by aggressors and victors as a justifiable, and in fact constantly justified, means of pursuing or protecting their interests. Interests which, as history teaches, have always had their roots in purely economic issues or, which is the same, in struggles for power. The temptation to resolve any conflict in terms of violence, persecutions and wars is unfortunately innate in man. It is the consequence of our species' inability to resolve conflicts by other means. This inability spreads from the intimacy of families, where the victims are often women and children, to the political arena and, from it, to the theater of international relations. Throughout hi-

story the victims of violence, persecution and war have been, and continue to be every day, innumerable. Human suffering caused by all forms of violence is literally and sadly ineffable, that is, unspeakable, unquantifiable, incomprehensible.

Even if we wanted to restrict our attention to the present alone, to today's world, we would not be able to compile an exhaustive list of the pain inflicted on man by man. At the moment there are, depending on the counting criteria, between thirty and forty active conflicts, some of which are decades old. Ancient civilizations and entire nations have been reduced to rubble, their inhabitants killed or forced to flee, their human rights have been trampled on, pacts have been betrayed, legal practices resulting from centuries of reflection and civilization have been ignored or bent, yielding once again to the logic of power. Just today, February 24, 2022, Russia invaded Ukraine in a war which, like all others, we know where and how it began, but whose end is unknown, a war in which a nation has been taken in painful grip of two opposing blocs, NATO with Europe on the one hand and Russia with its vassals on the other, a war that could have been avoided with more intelligence.

The fact that, due to persecution and wars, there have never been so many refugees and displaced people as today cannot, therefore, come as a surprise. The United Nations High Commissioner for Refugees currently reports 82 million of them. This is the highest figure ever recorded since data are available and only ten years ago it was half of what it is today.[8] To refugees and displaced people have furthermore to be added all those who decide to leave their countries for economic reasons, in the hope of finding elsewhere those dignified living conditions that are denied them in their countries, which are increasingly poor and increasingly populous. The proportion of the world population on the move is now comparable to the population of the United States or Europe.[9]

Both in the case of wars and in the case of economic migration, these are phenomena of historical significance, intended to affect history and to persist for generations. They are historical phenomena that will not be reduced or controlled except with a radical change in the economic and redistributive policies at the international level. These phenomena are the direct consequence of the ever increasing scarcity of resources, of the ever increasing accu-

---

[8] United Nations High Commissioner for Refugees, *Global Trends 2020*.

[9] We are speaking of 281 million people according to the International Organization for Migration (2020).

mulation of the still available resources in fewer and fewer hands and of a growing world population. Such phenomena will certainly not be stopped by physical or psychological barriers. What would be needed are quite different policies and investments in the countries of origin, with costs that no country wants to face. A further cause of migratory phenomena, albeit hitherto secondary, threatens to become the main cause within a few decades: the environmental degradation to which we are subjecting the planet on which we live and to which we all owe, in the most literal and concrete sense possible, our life.

5. While it is true that humanity currently lives above its ecological budget, using almost double of yearly available resources, it is also true that the abuse of resources is not uniformly distributed. To claim that all humanity equally participates in unsustainable development would be false. In the face of a large majority of people who consume little or nothing, there is in fact a minority of nations that on average use three, four or even five times what they should and there is a small global elite of multi-billionaires who, with superyachts, private jets and space trips, have a huge environmental impact

compared to the rest of their peers.[10]

Humanity exceeded the biocapacity of the planet in the 1970s and the idea of being in an unsustainable phase of development has now become a matter of course, a fact accepted by most with bored intolerance. What we fail to do, however, is to understand that such a situation is not something we can live with for long, as we can do with a bad habit or some sin on our conscience. Nor is it something that a skilled politician and some statistical tricks can hide indefinitely: it is a physical limitation. A physical limit that those who cause most environmental damage (and should therefore be the first to change their behavior) do not see and that all the others, its victims, cannot influence in any way.

If current estimates of future world population growth are correct, agricultural production will have to make a quantitative leap in the next thirty years. Feeding a population of between nine and

---

[10] In *Carbon Inequality in 2030*, a joint briefing note by Oxfam International and the Institute for European Environmental Policy (2021), it is predicted that in 2030 one percent of the richest in the world will cause emissions thirty times higher than those compatible with the target, agreed in Paris in 2015, to limit global warming to 1.5°C, while the environmental impact of the poorest half of the world will remain well below that level.

ten billion human beings in 2050 will in fact require significant growth both in terms of yield of already cultivated land and in terms of arable land.[11] Although theoretically possible, such progress is by no means certain, so that the earth may soon find itself in a position where it cannot provide food security for the world's population. At the moment one tenth of this, concentrated mainly in Asia and Africa, still suffers from hunger, while a third is affected by food insecurity.[12] At the time of writing, a dramatic and persistent drought is hitting the Horn

---

[11] During the High-Level Expert Forum held in Rome in 2009, the Food and Agriculture Organization of the United Nations (FAO) estimated that the increase in agricultural production needed to feed the world's population in 2050 had to be around 70% when compared to the production levels of the period 2005–2007. In this regard, see also the *Global Environment Outlook 2019 (GEO-6)* report of the United Nations Environment Program (UNEP): "Various global trends in food and agricultural production, including population growth and global well-being, will require an increase in agricultural productivity (between 60 and 120 percent compared to 2005 production levels)."

[12] FAO, *Food Security and Nutrition in the World*, 2021. Furthermore, the data on food security reveal a notable difference between men and women: the percentages referring to women are in fact typically ten percentage points worse than those reported for men.

of Africa threatening, amid general indifference elsewhere, the lives of millions of men and women in Ethiopia, Somalia and Kenya. Conflicts, climate change and economic hardships, recently aggravated by the SARS-CoV-2 virus pandemic, negatively affect access to healthy food, which is made even more difficult by rising food prices. The quantitative leap required to keep feeding humanity should, by the way, also be sustainable, that is, it should not further jeopardize the possibility of feeding future generations. This would imply the transition to innovative agricultural techniques and the renouncing of fertilizers and pesticides which in the medium to long term cause damage to the land, a trend that is not yet observable on a global scale.

There is also a further problem: agriculture already absorbs 70% of the fresh water available worldwide. How the agriculture of the future can produce much more food with it or, ideally, even with less water is still unclear. What is certain, however, is that already today two billion people do not have access to water that is not contaminated by products used in agriculture, by chemicals used in (or caused by) industrial production, by drugs or simply by wastewater, 80% of which is reintroduced into nature without having been adequately treated.

The problem of waste and the pollution caused by it (in particular by plastics, metals and various chemical elements) affects the whole of life on earth, with serious consequences on flora and fauna.[13] Traces of microplastics have even been found, for the first time, in human blood. The air we breathe is also affected by similar problems and it is estimated that its pollution is currently responsible for the deaths of seven million people a year.

Finally, that the use of fossil fuels has severe repercussions on the environment, health and global warming of the planet should not come as a surprise to anyone. However, their availability is limited and destined to become substantially uneconomic in the coming decades. That of coal already is, while in the space of twenty years first oil and then natural gas should reach the point of maximum production, their *peak*, and then decline. At the moment, however, their demand and use is still growing. Their combustion is one of the main causes of climate change due to the two greenhouse gases carbon dioxide and methane. Without dwelling on the multiple negative effects of the use of fossil

[13] According to UNEP (*GEO-6*) the current one is an era of human history extremely exposed to the risks deriving from chemical products. In fact, the production of ever new chemicals exceeds our ability to ascertain their impact on human health and planetary ecosystems.

fuels in terms of soil, water and air pollution, global warming is perhaps the greatest threat humanity faces from an environmental point of view. Caused by greenhouse gases, but also by other factors such as agricultural production, industrial production of steel and cement or deforestation, this phenomenon is responsible for the warming of the seas, the rising of their levels, the melting of glaciers and polar ice, the progressive desertification of the earth as well as for unprecedented and intense meteorological events with a strong destructive potential. What follows is a lethal combination for plant and animal life on earth, a reduction in the economic resources available to the populations impacted by climate change, risks of drought, food crises, further poverty, conflicts and migration.

Finis Terrae

So long as all the increased wealth which
modern progress brings goes but to build up
great fortunes, to increase luxury and make
sharper the contrast between the House of Have
and the House of Want, progress is not real
and cannot be permanent.
(Henry George, *Progress and Poverty*)

There is now a general consensus on the fact that
the gross domestic product is inadequate to measure social progress and development. The very
idea of progress should be better contextualized:
the undoubted advances in scientific and technological terms that are visible to all are in fact ac-
companied by extremely worrying environmental
degradation and a social erosion that affects even
the most stable liberal and democratic societies,
affected by a slow but increasingly clear drift
towards authoritarianism and conflictuality.

Throughout history we have come to a point where our way of life is no longer sustainable, that is, it cannot continue to be as it is today. Our societies and the very planet we live on are threatened by a level of injustice and conflict that questions not only our coexistence but, at worst, the very survival of our species on earth.

Looking back over the elements just discussed, we realize that there are two main causes of the unsustainability of our present: the level reached by accumulative processes and the overpopulation of the earth. The course correction that humanity will have to undertake must therefore address both causes simultaneously and have as its objectives both a social rebalancing and a reduction of our ecological footprint.

In the first case, it will be a question of pursuing a redistribution of wealth and access to rights and resources that will allow the rehabilitation of the economic, political and social fabric of the communities in which we live and a cooling of the tensions that afflict the international community. In the second case, we will need to go back to a sustainable development, one which allows the regeneration of natural resources through a reduction of the effects of the human presence on earth.

The struggle for equality, which is not to be understood in formal terms (*law is equal for all*), but rather concretely, in terms of equality of real political power, is the task that humanity will have to face in this historical phase. Political equality is the next step in the long struggle for freedom waged in past centuries by the generations that preceded us, a struggle that has allowed us to free ourselves from imperial hegemonies, from feudal and ecclesiastical lordships, from servitude and slavery and which still engages us today in terms of racism and discrimination of all kinds. At this historic moment, the struggle for the very survival of our communities, societies and nations calls us to a commitment to the real equality of men and women within and outside their national contexts. It is not a question of moderating and compensating for the effects of accumulation, but of addressing accumulation itself as such, reversing its tendency and effects. And, as in the past, the first step has to be done by the most liberal and culturally advanced nations and societies. It is these which must indicate the direction to all the others, so that the scientific and technological progress that they have been able to guarantee also becomes ideal, social, economic and political progress.

Correcting the disparities that make one man stronger than another in terms of economic-political power is in fact one of the primary tasks of politics. Maintaining and protecting these corrections is then the task of justice as a bulwark against the spread of real-life law and against excesses of power. There is no equality without independent justice capable of carrying out its social function as a counterweight to the power of government. In exchange for the balance of powers, of all powers, equality offers the great gift of freedom, of the greatest possible freedom in the maximum dignity that can be experienced by every single member of society. Freedom and dignity are synonymous. But let there be no illusion about it: freedom, like a functioning democracy or social justice, is never acquired once and for all. The accumulative processes, with their erosive potential, ceaselessly continue their work in favor of private and particular interests, continually trying to add wealth to wealth, power to power. Every form of equality and every freedom is thus constantly threatened from within and from the outside of the social assembly and must therefore be constantly defended, regained and expanded generation after generation. There are four weapons to protect freedom: information, speech, action and resistance. Compassion is their source and each

generation will have only that freedom for which it
will be ready to fight.

The duty that I owe to the whole human race is
more primary and pressing than the one
I owe to a single man.
(Seneca, *On Benefits*)

1. Everything public is political. Everything that
happens in the public space, which involves the
communities in which we live, is a fact in itself and
immediately political, that is, concerning our way
of living together. This statement has two consequences. The first is that politics, as a discourse on
and government of the *res publica* (our common
wealth), has the right and the duty to deal with everything that is public by its very nature, since it is
relevant for coexistence in society. The second and
no less important consequence is that everything
that is private is and must remain excluded from
the political sphere.

The first objective of politics, as an activity regulating coexistence in the public space, is the well-
being and happiness of society as a whole. This im-
plies guaranteeing freedom, justice and peace for
all, together with protection, education, health and

a future worth living. The fact that political activity always involves the exercise of power and that power favors and is a vehicle for accumulation has contributed to the trend that social inequalities, rather than decrease, increase with economic inequality. There can be no equality among men in an economically unequal society: the poverty present in a society and the level of economic inequality are measures of the level reached by social and therefore also political inequality.

All policies that allow, facilitate or do not prevent continuous accumulation, that is, what is in fact a continuous redistribution of wealth from the bottom to the top of society, are therefore harmful to society as a whole, to the individuals who are their victims, to the planet that is plundered by them. The policies of accumulation are never centered on the public interest, but only on the individual interest.

Unfortunately, no politician today seems to have and propose a long-term vision. What prospect does he or she have for the next fifty or one hundred years? Where does he or she want to take the society they want to govern, what is the direction in which to work? Everything that professional politicians do and say is done and said in such a way as to maximize their chances of success in the next elections and are thus very short-term thoughts and actions, as well as obviously personally interested. And this circumstance is both a renunciation of the future and a renunciation of changing those social distortions that have afflicted the social body for decades, if not centuries. If the political horizon reaches only up to the next electoral round, there is no way to undermine the existing balance of power, which, on the contrary, constitutes the forces to befriend in order to secure a further and possibly better mandate. This kind of politics is equivalent to looking at your toes while walking in small steps, always and only worried about the next foothold. It is impossible to have a social vision under such conditions. But it is precisely this raising of the eyes that is needed to have a view of the horizon and to intelligently decide in which direction to proceed. This is what societies always need and what politics has the duty to deliver.

To counter the social disintegration to which accumulation and inequality lead, the few years between two electoral rounds are not enough. A long-term vision, courage and independence from the strong powers are needed. Politics has the task of protecting the whole of society and allowing everyone the free development of their human potential, in the respect and interest of the entire community. This requires both a balance between the powers of the institutions of the state and a balance between the powers of single individuals, so that those in a more fortunate situation than others cannot derive from their luck advantages that are detrimental to others or even to the entire community. Those who, because of their assets or the position held, by birth, good luck or personal ability, enjoy many more possibilities and power than others must also accept additional duties and limitations such as ensuring that their use of wealth and power can be publicly controlled (in the sense of being transparent and accountable) to ensure that it is not used to the detriment of the community. In other words, it is necessary to break the negative spiral that leads from accumulation to power and from this to an even greater accumulation which allows even more power. We need a social pact that balances wealth and power on the one hand and rights and duties on the other, which guarantees what could also be called *equal privileges*. Where this does not happen there is no justice and where there is no justice there is no true society, there is no feeling of common belonging, community, solidarity. In a functional society it is necessary to continuously preserve the balance and harmony of powers, wealth and opportunities. Any destructive, potentially antisocial and antidemocratic tendency, such as the centrifugal forces constantly generated by uncontrolled accumulative processes, must be fought and brought back into what is socially tolerable, i.e. not dangerous for the entire social body, for all members of the community.

Plato's unrealistic idea of entrusting the government of public affairs to philosophers without personal property, ridiculed by all subsequent critics, captures this important point. Whoever is or places himself at the head of a community must, as long as in this role, have such a level of moral and social intelligence as to place his personal interests in the background and to pursue in the first place, with all his abilities and with all his honesty, the interests of each individual member of the community. The exercise of the political office requires a spirit of duty, the capacity for humility and sacrifice, the clear renunciation, on the part of those who offer themselves to administer the common wealth, of what is admissible for private citizens: the search for personal success in terms of prestige and, of course, also in economic terms. And since this ideal has proved completely unrealistic throughout the history of the world, it must be institutionalized in legal terms.[14]

The point is not the abolition of private property (a dystopia) or the renunciation of it, much less that of the reduction of the freedoms of individual citizens, but a juridical and constitutional structure that guarantees the equality of the members of society in terms of real power. Just to give an example, electoral success in the United States depends on the availability of substantial electoral funds, often from extremely wealthy individuals or large corporations (a fact which, incidentally, has slowly transformed the US system from a democracy with universal suffrage into a plutocracy with hampered suffrage). In such circumstances it takes a lot of imagination to believe that the senators of that country pass laws that are to the detriment of their benefactors, that is, of those to whom they owe office, prestige and salary. Compensating for this institutional deformation would therefore require a law prohibiting particularly wealthy citizens or large companies from sponsoring individual

---

[14] Transparency International's *Corruption Perceptions Index 2021* underlines the strong correlation between political freedoms and respect for human rights on the one hand and transparency of public offices and services on the other. The most authoritarian and oppressive states are also the most corrupt and dysfunctional.

candidates or political parties in any form. Is this a restriction of the rights otherwise enjoyed by the rest of individuals and society? Certainly. But it is a restriction that aims precisely to safeguard the political equality of all citizens by balancing their real powers and which also aims to ensure that parliaments can truly represent the interests of society as a whole.

Further examples of legislation in this sense could be one where anyone who already has exceptional wealth (and therefore exceptional power) cannot hold public offices that would increase that power, or one where anyone who aspires to a public office of some importance must declare publicly the extent and source of their assets and income before, during and after the exercise of their office, in such a way as to guarantee absolute transparency to the electoral body regarding any conflicts of interest in the exercise of their public function. Other measures could target companies, economic sectors or even the work of lobbies, currently completely under-controlled.

The catalog of measures needed to guarantee citizens' equality in terms of real political powers does not necessarily have to be long and complex. Rather, it is necessary to establish guiding principles and to identify, also on the basis of the specific context, what legislation is necessary and sufficient to stop what is essentially always a distortion, an abuse of power by those who have that power or can with all evidence influence it. Only free societies, free from the risk of abuse, are solidary and functioning societies.

> When you beat the olives from your trees, do not go over the branches a second time. Leave what remains for the foreigner, the fatherless and the widow. When you harvest the grapes in your vineyard, do not go over the vines again. Leave what remains for the foreigner, the fatherless and the widow.
> (Deuteronomy)

> Take from their wealth a charity by which you purify them and cause them increase, and invoke Allah's blessings upon them.
> (the Quran)

2. There is only one way to counterbalance the damage created by accumulative processes in social, political and economic terms: a constant, certain and adequate net transfer of wealth from top to

bottom, from those who have been able to take advantage of the accumulative processes to those who have become the victims of such processes.

The absence of effective corrective measures to protect the community from the consequences of accumulation is not due at all to the inability of the political classes, but rather to the propagated vision of society in which men are substantially unequal and must remain so. Whoever has more power and wealth, so the underlying idea, deserves it and has to be allowed to keep it. In the past, inequality was justified with an appeal to the divine will. More recently it has been explained by the invisible, but substantially just, hand of the market. And, always, this idea and this inequality have been defended with the weapons that power has been able to afford every time, whether these are the weapons of current law or those of the security apparatuses. But, beyond the narrative of the right difference (a background scenery), the political disinterest in balancing society keeping it healthy is structurally due to the alignment to the strong powers of those who have political responsibility (if not even, and very often, to their same complicity with those powers).

Private wealth and political connivance are the two great enemies of social justice, that is, of a society truly founded on the equality of its members in terms of real power. Any policy that has the *common wealth* at the center of its interests, that is, the social body as a whole, should instead have as its objective the fight against the excesses caused by the accumulative processes and their effects on communities: poverty, disparity, absence of solidarity, slow disintegration of the social fabric. In this sense, the first point in the program of any political party that truly cares about the fate of its community should be the abolition of poverty and the first question to ask every political candidate should simply be: "How do you intend to eliminate poverty and social disparity?"

On the basis of what distorted idea of equality are those who were born extremely rich allowed to become even richer every day while poverty still grips entire social strata, families and children? Rather it would be necessary (but here we are already moving on a platonic, ideal terrain) to introduce a limit to the politically tolerable accumulation, a limit that would bind permissible accumulation to the poverty that exists in the social context in question. Such a limit could be set high enough to allow the lucky ones to still feel (and still be) greatly privileged, but accumulation should not be allowed to proceed any further where the luck of the few would mean the bane of all others.

An effective top-down redistribution of wealth undoubtedly requires a lot of political courage but is also, and equally undoubtedly, fundable. The funds needed to support our societies and their institutions do not necessarily have to come from further debts or from continuous cuts to the welfare systems. Funds are there, they exist in abundance, but are concentrated in relatively few private hands. To combat social inequality and its effects, a policy of cuts in spending or public debt is not needed at all; what is required is instead a policy that has the courage to tap into the immense fortunes accumulated by the one percent of the population in order to reuse part of them for the well-being of the societies in which we live (and in which, incidentally, that one percent also lives).[15]

---

[15] By virtue of a rather bizarre psychological phenomenon, with reference to taxing great wealth, half of the population of industrialized countries feels threatened. It is as if even those who jog every now and then on a Sunday morning would feel directly impacted by changes to the Olympic Games' regulations. From this point of view it will certainly help to reassure the worried reader: if they do not have assets quantifiable in millions of euros or dollars, when talking about the rich we are not talking about them.

A first step in this direction is a much needed radical rethinking of tax systems, which should be based on assets rather than income in line with a simple principle: every member of the community has to contribute to social well-being on the basis of what society has allowed him or her to accumulate, that is, on the basis of one's assets. If 10% of citizens own 50% of private wealth, that 10% must also contribute 50% to the public costs necessary for the protection and development of the whole society. Any form of taxation or subsidy that does not take into account the patrimonial relationships between citizens is in fact equivalent to an upward redistribution. It is the ironic *stealing from the poor to give to the rich.*

Thanks to the incessant work of the accumulation processes, wealth in private hands grows constantly. Even in a year like 2020, in which state budgets have suffered from the ongoing pandemic, private assets have grown (and not just marginally).[16] Fur-

---

[16] The recent *European Wealth Report* by the research and consultancy firm Redesigning Financial Services concludes for instance that, while the gross domestic product of European countries contracted by 6.4% in 2020, private wealth reached an all-time high of 69 trillion euros, growing by 3.9% in the same period and at the same time increasing the economic gap between wealthy and less well-off citizens: "Wealth is increasing-

thermore, the current unequal distribution of assets would mean that if the myriad of taxes and levies in force today for everyone on everything were replaced with a single tax on assets, only a small part of the population, the much richer one, would have to pay more than is currently the case. For the vast majority of people, moving from the current fiscal chaos to a single wealth tax would ultimately prove financially beneficial, as well as a definite relief in terms of bureaucracy and, hence, quality of life.

With the exception of the small minority of dictators, oligarchs and billionaires, a harmonious, balanced and functioning society in which all men are equal to each other in real, social and political terms is in fact in everyone's interest. And those who have had the misfortune of being victims of the accumulative processes, or the inability to adapt to them, should not be seen (nor should they perceive themselves) as beggars who live only thanks to the benevolence of the state and fellow citizens: poverty is a political, social and economic crime. It is a crime committed by a state accomplice of the

---

ly concentrated. The wealthiest 10% of European households make up no less than 51% of total net European wealth. The wealthiest 1% of Europeans occupy 19% of total European wealth."

strong powers, of private interests, and whoever happens to be poor is the victim of that crime, a victim who must be compensated. This is, by the way, precisely the meaning of the Islamic precept of *zakāt*, which is not a thankful almsgiving by those who have enriched themselves, nor a voluntary act of liberality, but a Koranic obligation, a law, and precisely the obligation to *purify* (a very meaningful term) their wealth through the transfer of part of it to the weakest members of society, widows, orphans and the poor in the first place. Poverty is legalized injustice. A side effect of accumulation, it is and remains a symptom of injustice. Not being poor, therefore, is a right and every human being has the right not to live in poverty.

In this sense, it is also necessary to rethink the whole system of subsidies and aid for those in economic difficulties. The general principle should be to guarantee each individual his financial independence, giving him full dignity and a role equal to that of any other member of the community in which we live. Dependence on aid, subsidies and social safety nets is neither dignified nor just. It reduces those who are less fortunate than others into a state of physical and psychological submission which makes them victims a second time of the economic and political system to which they happen to belong. A minimum basic income, unconditionally guaranteed to every citizen at risk of poverty, not only reduces poverty itself, but has positive effects on the health of the people who receive it, reduces the levels of domestic violence and crime, improves the school performance of the children who are rescued from poverty and, moreover, studies and experiments show that it is even advantageous for the public budgets: it costs less to guarantee those in difficulty a minimum income and to provide them with a place to sleep than to manage such forms of poverty with the usual mix of controls, assistance and social benefits.[17] But even if this were not the case, even if the elimination of poverty were not less expensive than other coping solutions, it would still remain just, dignified and a moral duty. And that is what matters. In the end, even those who are poor consume and, as consumers, contribute to the economic life of society. This contribution must be honored by those who, thanks to it, continue to enrich themselves.

Italy is a democratic Republic founded on labour.
(*Constitution of the Italian Republic*)

---

[17] On this point see for example Rutger Bregman, *Utopien für Realisten*.

3. One of the most beautiful wishes of the Italian language is *Buon lavoro!*, the wish for a job that challenges, but also offers satisfaction and a reason for pride, which justifies the time spent at work and ennobles the evening tiredness.

Unfortunately, not everyone has the opportunity to find satisfaction in a good job. In a world where forms of slavery and exploitation (including sexual exploitation and the exploitation of children)[18] still persist, where many nations suffer from endemic unemployment and do nothing to guarantee acceptable wages, in which even those who work full time can remain poor,[19] only a minority can claim

---

[18] According to estimates by the International Labour Organization, in 2016 some 40 million people, most of them women, worked in conditions similar to slavery. Of these 40 million a quarter were children. *Global Estimates of Modern Slavery: Forced Labor and Forced Marriage*, 2017.

[19] The phenomenon of working poverty is a burning social issue in the United States, but it is not limited to that country. In their article *More Than Just Nickels and Dimes: A Cross-National Analysis of Working Poverty in Affluent Democracies* (2010), David Brady, Andrew Fullerton and Jennifer Moren Cross analyze the phenomenon in economically advanced democracies, reaching the conclusion that, although in the United States eleven percent of the population lives in poverty

to have a decent job. Even fewer, much fewer, are those who can say they have a fulfilling job, one which satisfies them, which fulfills them humanly. The search for work originates from need and the need generates dependence, dependence of the worker on it and on whom can satisfy that need. The need to work submits the worker to the one who can offer a job, so that a society in which unemployment is high and in which the need for work is barely satisfied is a society of citizens reduced to servitude, forced to hope and beg for a job that allows them to feed their families. Societies characterized by enormous social inequalities always have a labor market in which need reigns and in which work takes the form of more or less voluntary slavery. High unemployment, a sign of a high level of social need, is always also the symptom of serious social dependence and therefore, literally, also of a great lack of freedom in terms of real political and civil equality.

But there is more. Not only does the need to work materially, psychologically and politically submit the worker to his employer – not only by working,

despite having a job, other economies are also not exempt from the problem. In Italy, for example, the working poor are more than seven percent of the population, which is more than half of the total poor (twelve percent).

the worker contributes to enriching those who have employed him – but the work itself, the commitment necessary in it, absorbs attention, energy and time: year after year, work weakens and consumes the worker who, understandably, will devote his free time to rest, family and consumption. There is not much time left for anything else, for example to pursue one's personal development and improve one's job prospects. Nor are there many energies left to reflect on society and the role workers play in it, for critical and lucid thinking at the same time. The need, the work meeting that need, and the working activity of man are thus functional to accumulation itself, forms of its reproduction and growth.

Even in a free and egalitarian society work is needed, of course. But in it, work is not dependence, it does not generate servitude. The freer the job market is from need, the freer is the society, because liberation from dependence makes the workers citizens with full right of choice. In such a society the need to work, the demand for jobs, is lower than the vacancies generated by companies, unemployment is minimal, workers have a wage level guaranteed by law that frees them from need, and they work under conditions and with contracts that maximize their freedom of choice, movement, employment and personal development.

For this to happen, the political and social asymmetry generated by the need for work must be counterbalanced by labor laws that decrease the rights of employers and increase those of the employees by what is necessary to make both equal in terms of real social power. In such a society, in a society founded on the real equality of employers and employees, every worker, whatever the specific form of his employment is, always remains a free worker.

The pace and scale of the required economic transformation is unprecedented.
(OECD, *Investing in Climate, Investing in Growth*, 2017)

4. Our current model of life, based on the consumption of what exists, is not sustainable. By continuing to live as we do today we are condemning future generations to a miserable existence, marked by uncertainty and emergency.

In this respect it is therefore necessary to adapt our lives to the ecological budget at our disposal, that is, to return to a sustainable economy and consumption. This requires huge structural changes which, however massive, will become increasingly difficult to manage the longer we wait. Not only because the damage caused by the ongoing processes will increase, but also because in the meantime our ability to respond and react to the situation will decrease.

Smart and sustainable consumption will only be possible where the whole of society is adequately educated and aware that this is the only way forward. It is a question of reducing the production of artifacts by reducing the need for them, encouraging the renunciation of the superfluous as well as the reuse, repair and recycling of what we already possess.

In this sense, it is necessary to introduce increasingly stringent industrial and social sustainability targets and to rationally abolish all subsidies for activities that contribute to pollution and environmental degradation. Each industry will have to optimize its processes, to reduce the resources used and not to cause further damage to the planet through the products it markets for its own profit.

Ideally, every human activity, industrial as well as social or individual, should quickly be adapted so as not to leave any environmental footprint, that is, to have a neutral or even positive environmental balance. Renewable resources must be increased, not reduced or threatened, and non-renewable ones must be replaced as soon as possible by innovative technologies which reduce our dependence on what will soon no longer be available to us.

On the way to a positive environmental balance, it is necessary to ensure that always and everywhere whoever causes environmental damage is liable financially and, if necessary, also criminally. The *polluter pays* principle must be applied without exception to institutions, companies and individuals. And the revenues that come from the taxation of polluting activities must be reinvested in environmental activities.

On the international level, it is necessary to establish an international environmental governance that takes into account the fact that resources such as air, water, forests and arable land and problems such as pollution and climatic risks are issues affecting humanity as a whole. Under an international environmental authority, financed by all the nations of the earth, areas or activities of particular humanitarian and ecological importance should be managed, protected and even developed in accordance with the most current scientific knowledge. It should be accepted that entire areas of the planet, such as the Amazon rainforest for instance, are protected through supranational funds and authorities, and not left to the political interests and economic difficulties of a single country. If environmental problems are a threat to the whole of humanity, it is the entire international community that has to deal with them, and the sovereignty of individual states must, in this sense, be limited on the one hand (in terms of negative decisions) and financially supported on the other (in terms of compensation).

The sustainability of life on earth is neither a political option nor a luxury that we can give up. Threatening our very survival, the environmental issue is, together with those of social equality and peace, a priority political issue. If economic processes and lifestyles need to be radically changed to save us, let this happen. Otherwise not only will the economy itself risk returning to bartering, but the whole of humanity will have to fight for mere survival.

5. The rebalancing of individual national societies should then be complemented by a radical rethinking of international policies. Since the beginning of history, almost every war has been dictated by the desire to get hold of other people's resources in terms of territories, resources or human lives. The entire history of the empires of antiquity or of

medieval conquests, of colonialism, of military imperialism of the early twentieth century and of current geopolitics is marked by the hunt for resources and markets dictated by industrial interests, and therefore ultimately by private purposes, rather than due to real collective needs. Nothing has changed, in this sense, from the Second World War to today. Every conflict always arises from concrete and opposing interests in terms of power, wealth and resources, and he who wants to understand its true nature just has to look at the commercial and financial flows that precede and follow the conflict.

Until after the Second World War, however, no conflict has ever threatened our very survival as a species. The massacres that a part of humanity has regularly inflicted on the enemy side have never had consequences for the whole of humanity. With the advent of the Cold War, all of this changed. Not only because a possible nuclear war would have concrete possibilities of decimating life on earth for entire centuries, but also because we no longer have the time to think about war on a planet whose resources are diminishing day by day. Even without the use of weapons of mass destruction, every single conflict steals resources, as well as precious time and intelligence, from the only battle worth fighting: that for the salvation of the planet that hosts us.

We need to move from our national security architectures, based on our respective alliances and military forces, to a world peace architecture guaranteed by international agreements and mutually balanced defense mechanisms. Once put in place and functioning to everybody's relief, we should then move on to a second phase whose objective would be a progressive plurilateral disarmament, a constant, controlled, reciprocal reduction of armaments in order to reduce the destructive potential of wars and, above all, to increase mutual trust and collaboration, while at the same time freeing up significant economic resources for other purposes. A third phase could eventually be constituted by the creation of international agencies that take on the rational management of resources, transposing it from contrasting national logics to a collective perspective. A reform of the United Nations, already a dire necessity today, could at that point also become realistic and welcome.

We are still a long way from all this. And yet these three steps could be accomplished within three generations, in the span of a century that would transform the history of humanity from a chronicle of bloody conflicts into a path towards building sustainable coexistence.

Only by leaving the national logic will we be able to rethink and change current policies and, for example, stop tolerating and corrupting bloody regimes in Africa only to better plunder its territories. And only by resolving the crises that we ourselves cause on these continents will we be able to resolve the vicious circle of crises and migrations that are increasing every year and that threaten to completely disrupt the world as we know it today. Migratory flows are the symptom of the imbalance we have created and require a coordinated response on several levels: if on the one hand it is necessary to help those who, out of desperation, find themselves in immediate need of humanitarian aid, on the other hand it is necessary to stabilize the societies from which these flows depart, so that those who would prefer it will have the option of staying in their own country and those who want to leave will have the hope and the legal means to do so without putting themselves and their family in danger. In the long run, however, the political and economic conditions of the countries of origin must have changed for the better, and if it is our own policies causing that imbalance, then we must eliminate its causes in our system and repair the damage done by our society to the others. We cannot exploit a country by corrupting its political class, stealing its resources, reducing it to a state of necessity and insecurity and then refusing to accept the consequences of our actions and not taking care of and assisting those we have forced to flee with our predatory behavior.

Protecting what we have today and what we have achieved throughout history can no longer be based on an ever greater exploitation of others or an increasingly fierce competition between nations, because this method has reached its limits and the crises we cause elsewhere backfire on us without delay. The world is now more connected than ever, and what once were huge distances between continents and communities have become routes that can be covered in months, if not weeks. There is no *elsewhere* far away any longer, everything is so close and interconnected that we ourselves are both profiteers and victims of our struggle for resources. Therefore, protecting what we have and what is essential to us requires instead a real, open cooperation with our fellow men, and the protection not only of our own, but also of all other societies.

This goes hand in hand with the resolution of the forty armed conflicts currently underway, to be resolved through international commitment and guarantees as well as, why not, also through more creative political solutions than seen in the past. Why not share the administration and sovereignty of disputed territories, for instance? If peace and prosperity are real priorities, then we must devise new political models to jointly address and resolve the causes of conflict together. With the reduction of wars, with the creation of demilitarized areas or regions or with the delegation of the management of strategic resources to multilateral organizations guaranteed and controlled in their own autonomy, what must be achieved is essentially a rethinking and a redefinition of the concept of sovereign state as we know it today. In a pacified world, the competition between states, and therefore that *otherness* that justifies their existence by contrast, must transcend its current form to become a cultural phenomenon, rather than degenerate into a source of conflict. Before countries like France, Italy or Germany were unified in their present form, various and sovereign territories coexisted in them in a constant mutual struggle. Of them, of their glory and pride, remain today only folkloristic vestiges or, at best, precious and appreciable cultural heritages. Nothing else is required today than hasn't already happened in the past: what we must be able to take is a further step from a competitive local logic to a cooperative logic strategically based on our common interests and centered on international peace and justice.

All this may sound extremely naive. So be it. But without a stable and just distribution of resources on the international level we will face increasingly disastrous wars in terms of human lives and material costs. Wars which, moreover, will involve us immediately, having a direct impact on our lives. Without stable and just international policies our communities will find themselves on the front line every day and there will no longer be a way to avoid wars that involve everything and everyone in a vortex of suffering and mourning. In an interdependent world like the present one, it certainly won't be the next war that saves us. Only peace can guarantee a further expansion of our respective societies. If this does not happen, guaranteeing security, freedom, justice and well-being within and outside our communities may soon prove impossible. And, in the worst case, simply superfluous.

The rich and privileged, when also corrupt and incompetent, do not accept rescuing reform. Lack of intelligence is an undoubted bar.
(John Kenneth Galbraith,
Economics in Perspective)

6. Between humanity and its future there are two major obstacles: the resistance of those who have taken and continue to take advantage of historical accumulation and the overpopulation of the planet.

One of the tragedies humanity is dealing with at the moment is the myopia of the classes which continue to derive enormous profits and power from the accumulation process. Those who dominate economics and politics have not yet understood that they too will not be able to save themselves by appealing to the figures printed on their bank statements if the logistical and vital infrastructure built by humanity over the past two centuries ceases to function. Already now our daily life essentially depends on the interconnection of machines and databases that require constant maintenance and a reliable supply of energy. And, as always, our very physical survival depends on an adequate supply of food and the availability of drinking water, two factors that are neither obvious nor guaranteed in contexts that have entered a threatening crisis. A world in which infrastructure collapses and logistics systems fail will offer no chance of survival even to the industrial, financial or political elites. Just as the French nobility of the ancien régime had a last chance to save themselves, but did not take it, opting instead for their own bloody extinction, so also those who today travel around in huge private yachts and in personal spaceships will, in the face of a planetary crisis triggered by their own greed or stupidity, have to deal with a reality in which simply surviving will already be a success. It is easier for a camel to go through the eye of a needle than for a rich man to enter the kingdom of God: it would be good to help him.

The second major obstacle is of a different nature. Even if the majority of governments managed to agree on how to curb global warming and even if, beyond that, the commitment was kept, two rather unlikely hypotheses at the moment, this would only be a first step towards the solution of the environmental problems that we have already created. Even with climate change under control, the planet's non-renewable resources will run out more and more quickly, while the renewable ones (air, water and earth) are degraded by the pollution that the lives of eight billion people and a growing industrial production cause on a daily basis. The planet we live on is unable to provide for the existence of so many human beings. And while billions of men try to improve their living conditions, those who already have had the luck to live comfortably will not give up an existence that is incompatible with the future of the earth. Returning to a historical phase of sustainable development requires therefore a drastic change in our lifestyles, but also the reduction of the world population to a level able to provide for its needs with only renewable resources, thus allowing the planet to recover from the disease that our needs and our daily consumption represent.

The alternative is not rosy: given that the planet cannot offer much more than what is already being taken away from it day after day, either the population living on the planet decreases, or its needs (in terms of nutrition, health, longevity, work, transport etc.) will have to. It goes without saying that a decrease in the world population cannot and must not be pursued through legal prohibitions and impositions. Births decrease in a completely natural and voluntary way as soon as men and women, especially the latter, have the opportunity to receive an adequate education and to emancipate themselves.

Education and, in particular, the cultural, social and financial emancipation of women is a precondition for the survival of our civilization. Those societies and cultures that still prevent women from living alongside men in a status of absolute equity effectively renounce half of their human potential and not only inflict and make themselves guilty of daily violence and suffering, but are destined to an ever greater delay in their own development, to an ever greater collective misery. The future of every society depends on the liberation and the unfolding of the potential of all discriminated and marginalized social groups and, first and foremost, on the emancipation of women. Without the liberation, the intelligence and the active contribution of all women we will not have any hope of protecting the planet and our well-being with it.

> Sustainable development is a process of change in which the exploitation of resources, the direction of investments, the orientation of technological development; and institutional change are all in harmony and enhance both current and future potential to meet human needs and aspirations.
> (*Brundtland Report*, 1987)

7. *Finis terrae*, the end of the world, is a deliberately misleading title, as it refers solely to the world seen through the eyes of men. The announced end is, in reality, the end of our civilization in its present form. It is our future that is at stake, not the earth's. It is only the earth of men in the form in which we built it, the millennial Tower of Babel,

which threatens to disappear forever because of our greed. Nothing else.

I have no doubt about the survival of nature as such. Of course, if we do not change our way of thinking, living and acting, many animal species will become extinct. Many plant species and entire habitats will disappear. But nature, as a cosmic force of generation and regeneration of worlds and beings, cannot be stopped. Nature is the cosmic clock, much larger than us, in which everything will continue to move, to change and to evolve. With or without us. It is energy in constant motion. It is time itself. And it is only a matter of time, perhaps even a long time, but what we drag with us into ruin will leave room for new forms of life that will reproduce and multiply again, without rest.

Living in Africa, in a city built badly and in a hurry, in the midst of nature, I do witness every day of how man must defend his habitable space from vegetation and animals of all sorts that are waiting for nothing else but our distraction, or prolonged absence, to take back the spaces that we have stolen from them. If the place where I live were to be abandoned altogether one day, in a couple of decades it would be regained by what we struggle to keep under control and in the span of half a century everything that has been built here would be claimed by a nature that has neither mercy nor cruelty, but is simply unstoppable. The remains of humanity abandoned here would be swallowed up by it, digested and then reintroduced into the cycle of life in new forms.

Of course, a planetary ecological catastrophe would have a completely different scale. The whole planet would be involved, every form of life on it would falter. But who could believe in all seriousness that this would stop, and forever, the course of nature itself? If this same entire planet were to become a victim of our stupidity, what would this hugely sad event mean in the face of the immensity of the universe? Nothing ... absolutely nothing would have happened.

Our civilization has made great strides in the last millennia, but the greatest power we have come to in this very short glimpse of cosmic time is to be able, without actually having much more to do now, to self-extinguish ourselves. It is perhaps a self-defense mechanism of nature, which provides that an animal species at the height of its power destroys itself. Or maybe we really live in the best of all possible worlds, i.e. in a world where the worst enemy of the planet is gently led by nature itself, over the course of its evolution, to voluntarily step aside.

History or, rather, our history is coming to a major bend in the road. The sooner we prepare to negotiate it, the better. By speeding and happily accelerating, as we are doing now, that turn will not disappear from the road, but it will simply become more and more difficult to deal with, to the point of putting our very life at risk. Avoiding the catastrophe that threatens our world, our civilization and everything each of us holds most dear is, however, still in our power, and there is no doubt that, once cornered, we will take all necessary measures to protect ourselves. These, however, will become more and more onerous, dramatic and with an uncertain outcome the longer we wait. The question is therefore not whether we will change pace and the development model, but when, at what price and with what chances of success. How long will we be waiting?

We know what doesn't work and we know what it takes:

- An effective abolition of poverty, i.e. the recognition of the right not to be poor and the adoption of all necessary measures to reverse the socially negative tendencies of accumulative processes.

- Political equality, i.e. an active, concrete balancing of rights and duties on the one hand and real political power on the other.

- A wealth tax regime that allows nations to adequately meet social needs and to repay the debts incurred up to now.

- The defense and constant expansion of individual freedoms and civil and political rights, fundamental to guarantee the functioning of any liberal society.

- The real emancipation of women and of all social groups still subject to political, economic or cultural discrimination.

- A consistent, rigorous industrial and environmental policy based on the principle that the polluters pay for all the damage caused, as well as on our return to sustainable development.

- The transition from particular national approaches to security to a global architecture of cooperation, shared sovereignty and sustainable coexistence.

We know what's wrong and we still have the intelligence and strength needed to shape our destiny. But for this to happen we must not lose the ability to be indignant. Indeed, only by not losing our faculty of becoming indignant will we be able to take a stand and defend the freedom and plurality of the societies in which we live. We will have to act without delay, both in our private, particular sphere and in the public space that we will have to keep open to our opinions and our collective interests. We need to act quickly and together, all together, in justice.

He who doesn't seek the impossible
will not find it.
(Heraclitus)

Referenced Data

The data mentioned in the text originate from the most recent publications available from the following organizations:

Atelier BNP Paribas (atelier.net)

Food and Agriculture Organization of the United Nations – FAO (fao.org)

Freedom House (freedomhouse.org)

Intergovernmental Panel on Climate Change – IPCC (ipcc.ch)

International Labour Organization – ILO (ilo.org)

International Monetary Fund – IMF (imf.org)

International Organization for Migration – IOM
(iom.int)

Organisation for Economic Co-operation and
Development – OECD (oecd.org)

Oxfam (oxfam.org)

Redesigning Financial Services (redesigning-
fs.com)

Transparency International (transparency.org)

United Nations Environment Programme – UNEP
(unep.org)

United Nations High Commissioner for Refugees –
UNHCR (unhcr.org)

United Nations Organization – UN (un.org)

V-Dem Institute (v-dem.net)

World Bank (worldbank.org)

World Inequality Lab (wir2022.wid.world)